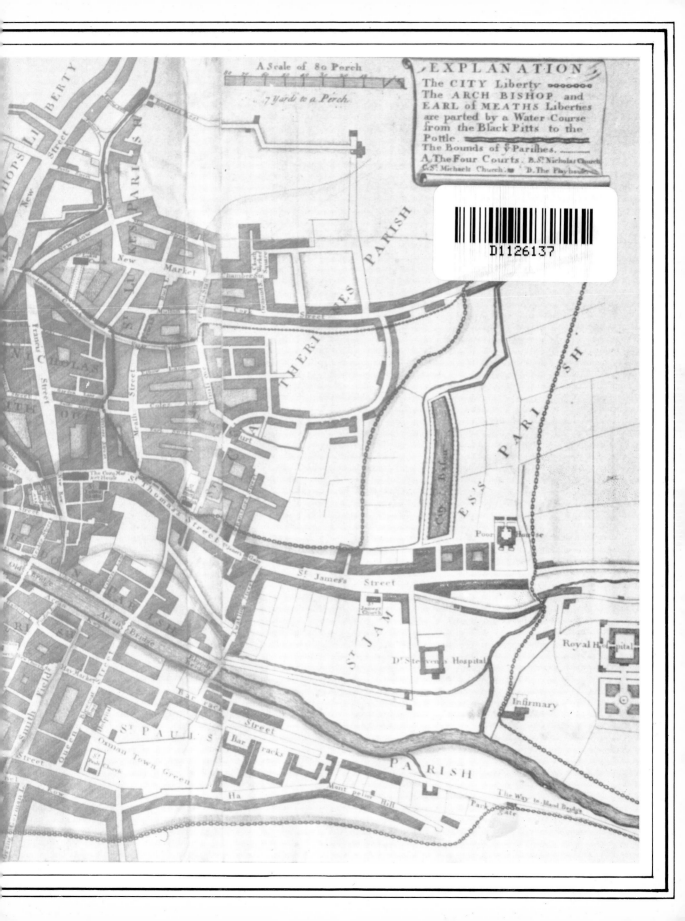

Princes & Pirates

To Judge Bill Bauer

Best Wishes

Dave Peerie

(President Dublin
Chamber of Commerce)
2004

L. M. Cullen

Princes & Pirates

THE DUBLIN CHAMBER OF COMMERCE 1783·1983

DUBLIN CHAMBER OF COMMERCE

1983

Text Copyright © 1983 L. M. Cullen

General Editor: Bernard Share

Designed by Jarlath Hayes.
Printed in Ireland by Brindley Dollard Limited,
Greencastle Parade, Coolock,
Dublin 5.

Published by
The Dublin Chamber of Commerce,
7 Clare Street, Dublin 2.

ISBN 0-900-346-49-3

Contents

Acknowledgements

The Dublin Chamber of Commerce wishes to thank Allied Irish Banks Ltd. for their generous sponsorship of the publication of this book and the contribution of many other Members to the project.

The editor wishes to record his indebtedness to the following: National Gallery of Ireland for illustrations on pps. 16 and 17; Irish Distillers (p. 23); Bank of Ireland (p. 36); Hugh Oram (p. 57); Miss Alice Shackleton (p. 78); Mr. Alex Findlater.

The Rt. Hon. the Lord Mayor Councillor Dan Browne P.C.

Mansion House
Dublin 2
Telephone 761845

There are many things that go to make up the life of a capital city: parliament and people, politics and religion, arts and entertainment, public services and private initiative; but no city can be said to be thriving unless its trade and commerce is in a healthy condition and in the hands of progressive individuals and organisations. Two hundred years ago, when the Dublin Chamber of Commerce was founded, our city had already laid the foundations of what was to become a major commercial and business centre, trading both within Ireland and with many parts of the world, stimulating the urban development that was to evolve into the capital of today.

It is a fascinating story, and one which every Dubliner, and many beyond our boundaries, will find full of interest. The changing fortunes of the Chamber down the years reflected the changing circumstances of the merchants themselves and thus of the community as a whole. Here are the famous names of Dublin commercial life _ the Guinnesses, the Powers, the Pims, the La Touches, William Martin Murphy and many others of yesterday and today _ and some of the less renowned who were content to serve the interests of an important institution, directing the considerable influence of the Chamber and its members towards improving conditions not only for themselves but for their city as a whole.

Dublin has expanded greatly in the course of two hundred years, but the city that would have been familiar to the promoters of the Dublin Chamber of Commerce remains recognisable in its essentials. Trade and commerce, and with it the unmistakeable character of Dublin life, is again flowing back into the Liberties, the cradle of the Community and of its mercantile development. As Lord Mayor, I welcome this renewal of the heart of our city, and I warmly welcome this history as a worthy record of the generations of enterprising Dubliners who helped to make us what we are.

DAN BROWNE P.C.,
LORD MAYOR OF DUBLIN

Sources

This note lists only the surviving records of the Chamber, not the range of sources on which this account of the Chamber is based. None of the letter books of the Chamber are known to have survived. After the Chamber left the Commercial Buildings in 1964, some miscellaneous material which the Chamber possessed was, at a later date, given to the National Library. The papers illustrate some aspects of both the city's and the Chamber's activities, but do not throw much light on the Chamber's own history. They are at present among the uncatalogued accessions of the National Library.

ROYAL IRISH ACADEMY.

MS.3C.25. Working minutes (sometimes signed) of Committee of Merchants, 1768-83 (1 vol.).

MS.12D.29 Minutes (unsigned) of Committee of Merchants 1767-82 (1 vol.).

CHAMBER OF COMMERCE, 19 CLARE STREET

Minutes (signed) of the Council of the Chamber of Commerce. 1783-1791, 1805-1807 (1 vol.).

Minutes (signed) of Council, 1821-1823 (1 vol.).

Working minutes, 1805-1809, 1 vol. (also contains minutes of meeting of 22 Dec. 1812 and partly torn minutes of 2 other meetings of same period).

PUBLIC RECORD OFFICE

Reports (printed) of Council to Annual General Meeting, 1821-1951 (17 bound volumes).

The series is not complete, but some early missing reports are among an incomplete set in the Chamber of Commerce. No report appeared for 1856.

Minutes (signed) of General Assemblies, 1820-1919 (2 vols.).

Minutes (signed) of Council meetings, 1823-1938 (19 vols.).

Public Image

Advertising in the contemporary sense did not develop until midway through the period covered by this book: our examples are therefore drawn largely from the early years of the present century. Each historic advertisement or other item of printed material has been sponsored by the relevant member firm of the Dublin Chamber of Commerce, and we thank them for their interest and support.

I

*The merchant community 1670*1760*

Dublin was transformed in little over a century from the 1670s. At that date it was a city of only about 40,000 people, a third of whom were crowded into the walled old town. Most of the remainder were to be found in two elongated districts, one in the valley of the Poddle, the celebrated Coombe, the other along Thomas Street, already centre of the grain trade and the grain-based industries. The rest resided beyond the bridge across the Liffey, just to the east of what was later called the Smithfield district, where cattle reached the city from the north midlands. As the city's walls were still intact, although they no longer served a defensive purpose, it retained many of the characteristics of a walled town. There was a clear distinction between the old town, some of it still consisting of cage-work houses from the sixteenth century, and the more modern housing in brick, already appearing within the city but more commonly outside the walled area. The spread of the city and the appearance of new houses, often with the gable facing the street, accelerated from the Restoration of Charles II in 1660. To the east of the walled town, in the previously unbuilt land reaching from the Castle to Trinity College, whole streets of new houses along regular thoroughfares running from Dame Street down to the Liffey began to appear. With the erection of a second bridge, Essex Bridge, in 1678, the pace of building on the north side of the city quickened as well. The line of Capel Street was laid down as an extension of Essex Bridge. This was well to the east of the older district, and over the following decades new streets were laid down in a regular fashion on lots which had once been a strand. On both sides of the Liffey the new streets to the east became the most desirable centre of living: gentry and merchants moved to them, and the older districts were increasingly taken over by the artisans engaged in textiles as the industry grew, and by noisome industries such as tanning.

In the 1670s Dublin would have been no larger than Edinburgh and not that much larger than Bristol — outside London the two most populous cities in Britain. Thereafter, the growth of Dublin was very striking. Already 60,000 in 1700, the population had risen to 180,000 a century later. In 1800 it was easily the second largest city in the British Isles: Edinburgh had only 83,000 and Bristol had fallen far behind. It was now one of the largest port towns in Europe. Bordeaux, for instance, the largest port in France, with a population of 60,000 in 1690, had only reached 111,000 in 1800; Dublin was larger than Cadiz or Hamburg, slightly larger than Lisbon, and almost as large as Amsterdam, the other great ports of the Western façade of Europe. London, in fact, was the only port which was sizeably larger than Dublin.

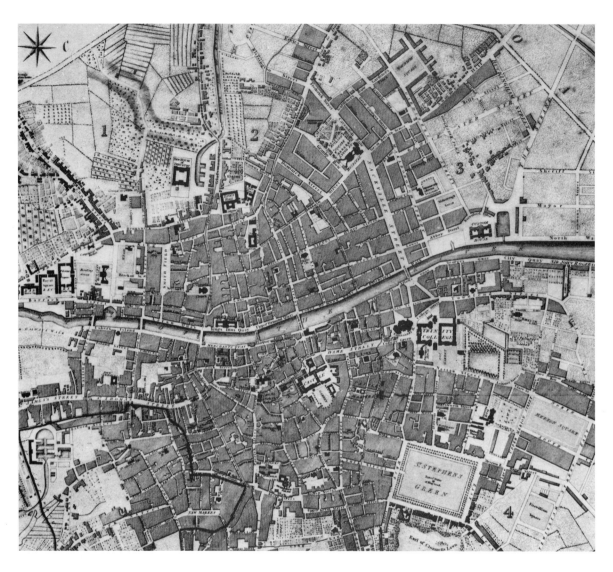

Dublin in the late 18th century. From a 1797 map published by W. Faden, London.

In the early decades of the century the city grew rapidly. The fashionable districts of the late seventeenth century filled in and by 1728 the centre of fashion had already moved further afield. On the Gardiner estate on the northern side Primate's Hill or Henrietta Street was laid out at this stage, and the city on the south side was beginning to fill in between Dame Street and St. Stephen's Green. As it grew the city continued to repeat a three-fold social division separating fashionable residence, commerce and industry. Merchants moved eastwards, in part because the building of Essex Bridge prevented ships coming up to the old quays; and as better-off residents left, workers in industry, especially the labour-intensive textile industries, took over houses, a family to a room. The 1710s and 1720s were a period of marked expansion in the city, where growth was now being expressed for the first time in a monumental manner. In the 1720s three enormous buildings were erected: the great library of Trinity, the splendid new parliament house — both in fashionable district created by Dame Street; and close to Henrietta Street on the northern fringe of the city's expansion at that time, the vast linen hall. The site of the linen hall was determined by its proximity to the roads from the north along which carts carried the linen cloth finished in Ulster to market. The streets around it were named after districts from which the cloth had come: Lurgan Street, Lisburn Street, Coleraine Street quickly filled up with lodging houses, coffee houses and businesses catering to the large population which frequented the linen hall. The fashionable development of the middle decades of the century, as in the past, progressed remorselessly east. Avoiding the increasingly commercialised high ground around Henrietta Street, it moved to lower lying areas of the Gardiner estate, where Gardiner Mall or Sackville Street took shape by 1750, followed by Rutland Square a decade later. On the south side, the fashionable district pushed to Dawson Street, acquiring prestige when the Earl of Kildare (the future Duke of Leinster), the grandee with the closest Dublin associations, built Leinster House, the finest of Dublin's stone houses, at the end of the 1740s. The prestige he conferred on his surroundings ensured that fashionable residence would cluster around his town house in a district which a short time before stood well outside the built-up area, and that in time fashion at large would move back from its northern refuge on the Gardiner estate to the south side. Merrion Square began to take shape from the 1760s onwards.

The pace of growth provided the need and occasion for planning the city's development. Moreover because it was dominated by the landed classes who gathered in parliament and resided in Dublin at least for a season, their interest in a fashionable and elegant environment provided the impetus for urban planning on a large scale. Dublin may be the largest and most sustained instance of urban planning in eighteenth-century Europe. For instance, its planning began earlier than that of Edinburgh and much of the new residential development was already executed before the New Town of Edinburgh began to take shape. The Wide Street Commissioners appointed by parliament began their work in 1757. Their first task was the creation of Parliament Street: it was intended to be the first street on the south side that visitors from the north side would encounter and was designed to sweep away the congerie of narrow streets and decaying houses which the visitor from across the river had to pass through before reaching the newer quarter around the parliament house. The very name the new street acquired — Parliament Street — signified its purpose. It anticipated many other works designed to create broad thoroughfares and elegant squares in the eastern districts as the landed and professional classes extricated themselves from the intense industrialisation and commercialisation enveloping the rest of the city. Even the newer streets leading to the Liffey were full of warehouses, and not a few chimneys like those of glass houses and process industries belched smoke and fumes. By 1760 both Rutland Square and the elongated line of Sackville Street or Gardiner Mall had already taken shape on the north side, and by 1790 Mountjoy Square had been laid out as a new square even further east and on higher ground. On the south side, Merrion Square was fully occupied by

Leinster House, the town residence of the Duke of Leinster, by James Malton, 1792.

houses by 1790 and Fitzwilliam Square was already laid out, although not built on. The planning of the new districts of Dublin was now substantially complete. By the 1780s the thrust of development of the residential districts on both sides was such that a bridge linking them directly, long mooted, seemed a pressing requirement, though the merchants had feared the building of such a bridge which would cut off their traditional district and quays from the sea. The decision in the 1780s to build was against their wishes and was the culmination of a dispute between merchants and aristocracy which had been simmering below the surface since the planning of the city had gathered pace in the 1750s.

Dublin had already come to dominate the country's overseas trade in the second half of the seventeenth century. At the outset of the eighteenth century over forty percent of Ireland's rapidly growing overseas trade was channelled through the capital, and this proportion rose to fifty percent in subsequent decades. Even new traffics were dominated by the capital. The huge linen trade which grew up in the eighteenth century, accounting for as much as sixty percent of total exports, centered on Dublin. The linen, woven and bleached in the north, was carried to Dublin in an unending stream of carts from April or May onwards until the end of the Autumn. The linen hall was opened in 1728 because the traffic was already based on Dublin: it was responsible for an enormous volume of business with buyers present from inland and from abroad. It also helped to account for the number of 'north country men' or northerners, mainly, but not exclusively, Presbyterian, who became merchants in Dublin in the course of the century. Dublin could never

The old Custom House, Essex Bridge, 1753, after J. Tudor.
Subsequently occupied by Dollard Printinghouse.

have developed attractive residential districts on the west side because that area was already highly commercialised even before the city began to spread rapidly. Smithfield and its cattle market and the barracks stood between the city and the attractions of the Phoenix Park and on the south side along Corn market, Thomas Street and James Street, the grain trade congregated, as did the largest of the breweries and distilleries which depended on the stream of grain and malt from the countryside. In this area itself there was

Dublin Bay with view of North Wall House, by Joseph Tudor, 1759.

17

an arresting division. Industries, which depended on imported raw materials were closest to the river side. Grain merchants, distillers, brewers and a host of traders in agricultural produce congregated on the line of Thomas Street and James Street mainly in housing of the eighteenth century. South of this line, in the valley of the Poddle, was a dense concentration of textile trades close both to customers in the city and to the food markets. The business districts themselves were thus highly stratified. Prestigious merchants like wine merchants whose clientele was in the upper classes moved east into Abbey Street or on the south side into Grafton Street and St. Stephen's Green. The great exporting and importing merchants congregated on the streets close to the river on both sides, especially on the south side from Eustace Street on to the warren of small streets between Usher's Quay and Usher's Island on the Liffey and the northern side of Thomas Street: these streets combined access to grain, malt and wool from the countryside and proximity to the coal brought up the river in lighters. Merchants, except for the linen trade, were less numerous on the north side, and many of them were in businesses purveying to the upper classes. Thus Abbey Street, along the frontiers of the Gardiner estate, became the major centre of the wine trade. The nerve centre of trade was of course the custom house quay itself. The custom house was at Essex Quay. The ships came up as far as the bridge, the masts of ocean going vessels over-shadowing it and reaching as high as the dormers of the custom house, itself a very tall building. At times, vessels were eight deep at the custom house quay, as ships sought to moor as close as possible to the commercial heart of the capital.

Dublin was not only a commercial and parliamentary city but an industrial city as well. Some industry always congregated in cities either because they contained most of the customers, as with brewing, or because, as with sugar, most of the raw materials came from abroad. Dublin was no exception. It had the largest brewing, distilling and sugar industries in Ireland: one third the output of legal whiskey and half the output of beer were manufactured in Dublin and about two-thirds of the sugar: there were about a hundred breweries, distilleries and refineries in the city in the second half of the century. These required as many business partnerships, and while some firms were small, many were large firms requiring substantial capital and managed by some of the richest members of the commercial classes in the city. The smoke and fumes of these premises hovered over the vicinity: the increase in their number and output was one of the factors driving the more fashionable and aristocratic members of Dublin society remorselessly to the east. However, if Dublin was quite like other large cities in its food and beverage industries, it was as a capital city quite unique in being the main centre of the textile industries, at least in wool and silk. In most countries these were based on smaller cities and increasingly were taking refuge in the lower-cost reaches of the countryside itself. Dublin ran against the trend of the eighteenth century. Its textile industries expanded at least until the 1770s: by that time they were probably the main source of support of perhaps not far short of 15,000 families, or about half the population. Textiles were dominated by master-manufacturers who employed a small number of looms squeezed into rooms in the crowded tenement houses. Textile workers were not well-paid, while at the same time the high costs of an urban textile industry meant that it was not particularly prosperous, Hence, inevitably, the industry occupied the cheaper districts which were being abandoned by the descendants of their original inhabitants and which had the least appeal either for commerce or residence. Thus the looms and the families who worked them, prepared the yarn for the loom or finished the cloth invaded houses built in the seventeenth or early eighteenth centuries but vacated as their former residents moved to more highly commercialised or more residential parts of the city. The economic vulnerability of these crowded districts where houses, often less than a hundred years old, deteriorated at an alarming rate, was reflected in acute misery in 1782-4 when commercial recession coincided with two years of harvest failure. In the 1790s, after more than a century of expansion, the textile industries were in decay. By the end of the century, even with cheap accommodation at a premium, some buildings and lanes were already derelict. The economic problems of its businessmen helps to explain why so many textile manufacturers and cloth merchants espoused political radicalism in the 1790s. In the United Irishmen there were no less than ninety-eight textile manufacturers and cloth merchants. On the other hand, merchants, benefitting as they did from the expansion of the city's general trade, were distinctly more conservative. Only thirty-two of the members of the Society were merchants — out of 400 or 500 in the city— and none of them was prominent with the exception of Mal O'Connor whose ties with the smuggling community in Rush on the coast of north Co. Dublin meant that he frequented a more radical milieu than most merchants.

Trade, manufacturing and parliament were the factors which in combination made Dublin an exceptionally fast-growing city, and turned it in the course of a century into one of the ten most populous in Europe. Only London, by far the largest city in Europe, had a similar combination of factors. Most European ports were not major administrative centres, and hence even the largest of them fared much less well overall than cities which dominated the administrative and political life of their country. Ireland's wealth concentrated in the hands of the landed classes. A group of perhaps around 2,000 families received about one sixth of the national income. In the 1770s this class must have had an average income of between £2,000 and £3,000 at a time when even the richest of merchants and manufacturers, with a handful of exceptions, earned much less than £1,000. Many of them were even .richer if the public offices and sinecures which they virtually monopolised were also taken into account: they were only rivalled in income by the most successful of the city's five-hundred-plus barristers. But successful barristers themselves came out of the landed class or turned wealth at the bar into land, and politics and litigation further bound up the bar inextricably with the landed classes. Up to four hundred members of the landed classes sat in the Irish parliament, three hundred in the Commons and some one hundred as peers, lay or ecclesiastical, in the Irish Lords. The spending of a high proportion of their income in Dublin was thus a powerful fillip to the city's service and luxury industries. Others among the gentry were attracted to Dublin during the social season which coincided with the sitting of parliament and was made dazzling by the presence of the country's parliamentarians. The latter were leaders of fashion, builders of

19

the greatest and first of its Georgian houses, and promoters of its public buildings from the linen hall and parliament house in the 1720s to the custom house in the 1780s. Some of the greatest, richest and most arrogant sat on the Wide Street Commissioners whose establishment coincided with a sharp rise in the self-confidence of the landed classes in the 1750s. Their incomes had risen sharply in that decade, as their rentals began to reflect the growth in trade in rural Ireland; they also won their political tussles with the lord lieutenant in the parliament in the 1750s, and overawed the administration.

In Dublin the landed classes were proportionately more powerful than in London because there the great corporations such as the Bank of England and the East India Company had created a financial milieu which had to be reckoned with and whose powers were distrusted by the more old-fashioned gentry in the countryside who had no links with them. In Ireland, in contrast to the pivotal role played by the city's capitalists in politics in London, the gentry lorded it over the merchant milieu. Dublin itself had no colonial trade of consequence. Cork had more, but the closest contact came from the Galway landed families who sent sons to the colonies and who also established relatives in Dublin as merchants. It is striking as a proof of the weakness of Dublin's colonial links that its sugar refining industry, one of the largest after London's in these islands, was built up not by local merchants who had colonial ties but by shrewd merchants from Bordeaux who had many ties with Dublin in the exchange of wine for beef and butter and who saw the prospects of developing them. Thus Dublin had quite literally a French sugar refining industry which did not draw at all on the personnel, capital or techniques of the industry which simultaneously was growing in the cities of Britain, and native businessmen, Catholic or Protestant, became prominent in the industry only late in the century.

Dublin banking grew not out of trade but out of the business of remitting the incomes of landowners from the countryside and holding their cash balances. Many of the Dublin banks were set up by landowners themselves or by agents who held their accounts. The first merchant banks were established around 1720 and merchants held only a limited share of the total banking business in the city. A decisive change seemed to be taking place in the early 1750s with the rapid expansion of merchant banks. The two biggest of these failed in 1745-55, an event which was followed in 1756 by an act of parliament which prohibited merchants engaged in foreign trade from conducting banking business. This was clearly an effort to re-establish the control of banking by the landed classes and to ensure subservience to their requirements. It was a humiliating treatment for the merchants, a measure which has no parallel in Europe at large in the eighteenth century. It was all the easier for the parliament to take the decision because one of the banks which failed had been Catholic, run by the Dillon family with links in London, Rotterdam and Bordeaux, and the other the Quaker house of Willcocks & Dawson which had mushroomed into the largest bank in the city. The significance of the act is underlined by the fact that it was followed in 1758 by the creation of an aristocratic bank run by three politician bankers, Anthony Malone, Nathaniel Clements and John Gore, all associated with the triumphant political grandees of the 1750s. It failed in 1759, but for the remainder of the century Dublin banking remained largely landed in origin and control. Only one new bank, that of Lawless and Coates, had an undoubted trade origin, its partners coming from a

20

Catholic and Quaker background. The major banks were all of landed origin or involved partnership with controlling landed interests. The bank of La Touche, mercantile in origin, turned into an aristocratic bank with little ties with trade, a change which accounted both for its prestige and success in the second half of the century. The subordinate role of merchants and bankers was thus clearly established, and the act of 1756 had a profound significance in shaping the relationship between the landed classes and business at large.

The rapid growth of Dublin, more rapid than that of most centres, meant that it was a magnet for men of ambition and ideas from all over the British Isles. Some of the English industrial cities, while as yet smaller than Dublin but eventually to become larger had a working class population and did not then or later offer a large market for luxury goods and services. Throughout the century there was an influx of artisans, traders, even hairdressers and the like from England, and from the 1770s a trickle of Scots, especially businessmen, also came into the city. The 1750s and the 1760s were the pinnacle of its development relative to cities elsewhere in the British Isles, and its attractions in that period were reflected in the fact that Sir George Colebrooke, a London financier and speculator, who had the dominant interest in the East India Company and was chairman, opened a bank in Dublin in 1764 which channelled money into his speculative adventures in London and which remained open until 1772. This confident growth of the Irish economy in the 1760s resulted in a speculative fever by the end of the decade; perhaps two-thirds of the money for Colebrooke's speculation came from Irish sources. The difficulties which culminated in his bankruptcy in 1772 were already anticipated in problems in his Dublin bank in 1770, and indeed bankruptcy took a severe toll of the Dublin business community in the years 1770-72.

If Dublin attracted outsiders, ranging from the Huguenot sugar refiners of the south-west of France in the 1720s to Colebrooke in the 1760s, it also enticed many Irishmen from the provinces. A very important stream was that of northern Presbyterians who came steadily to Dublin as the linen trade multiplied the links between the capital and the north-east. The Boyds and Kers were important early settlers; the Blacks came later in the 1760s, a progression which made sense because the family were long involved in the wine trade in Bordeaux and also moved in the 1760s into linen bleaching. The Dicks settled in Dublin at about the same time; linen was the basis of their interest and the importance of their business was reflected in the establishment of a branch in London and in governorship of the Bank of Ireland in 1797-9. A second stream were Quakers. Arthur Young in 1780 exaggerated the place of the Quakers in Irish business life. They were not numerous and only a handful of them were rich. A few like Fade and Willcocks had already made their mark, and the rapid growth of the yarn trade brought others, some of them from wool-combing districts in the midlands, to prominence in the 1750s and 1760s. Pims, Strettels and Coates all began to play a prominent role at this time and Abraham Wilkinson, who had a Quaker background, was also a major figure in the yarn trade. Coates in conjunction with a Catholic, Lawless, who conformed to the established church, opened the first and only bank in the hands of non-Anglicans after

David Digues, a French-born Dublin merchant who subsequently took the family name of La Touche. Founder of La Touche's bank, c.1719.

the debacle of Catholic and Quaker banking in the 1750s. Young was wrong in suggesting as he did that Quakers were the only large and dedicated merchants in Ireland, but the handful of Quakers were very prominent. Perhaps what impressed him and what he meant to say was how other merchants, many of them of landed background, espoused landed rather than mercantile values. The Pims were to remain the most enduring of the Quaker houses, and, unlike some families such as the Wilkinsons or Strettels, were also never to cease to be Quakers. John Pim settled in Dublin from the midlands during the boom in worsted yarn, and though he moved to London for business reasons around 1770 other members remained in Dublin. By 1790 the Pims were heavily involved in finance: they were the Dublin agents of many provincial houses, and they could certainly have progressed into banking but for the restrictions posed by the banking act of 1756. It is easy to see why Joshua Pim was one of the two Dublin merchants who drew up a plan for a chamber of commerce to defend their interests in 1783.

Catholics were not particularly numerous among the merchants in the city, but as with the Quakers the success of several of them was outstanding, creating the impression among some observers that they were more numerous than they actually were. As in the case of Quakers the middle decades of the century when business soared had been crucial for their emergence as a successful group in the city. Anthony McDermott was already prominent in 1761, and several other houses, like those of Blake, Byrne, O'Brien, Cosgrave and O'Connor came to the fore shortly afterwards. Catholics, like the Quakers, had very distinctive provincial and family origins. If many of the Quaker houses came from a handful of families in the midlands, the Catholics tended to spring from the younger sons of landed families in the west. Kirwan, Bodkin, Lynch, Blake emphasise the Galway origins of some of these houses, just as McDermott, O'Connor and McDonnell point to a background among the surviving landed Catholic families in Mayo/Sligo/North Roscommon for several others of the city's business families. One other source of Catholic mercantile success in Dublin came from Wicklow and north Wexford. As late as 1798 many Wexford rebels were able to go into hiding after the rebellion in the houses and businesses of Wexfordmen in the capital. The Byrne family in particular drew on a whole network of marriage and blood ties in Wexford, Wicklow and even Bordeaux. Through the marriages of the children of Thomas Sutton, a Wexford financier in Paris, they were linked to the McCarthy house in Bordeaux and to the financial house of Andrew French in London. It was this rich financial backing which explains why from relatively modest origins Edward Byrne, married to a McCarthy daughter, could rise in time to be the richest merchant in Dublin. The success of this house was to carry forward into the nineteenth century. Byrne's partner from 1788 was Randal McDonnell, and even when a Protestant-backed Chamber of Commerce was launched in 1805, years after the demise of the first one, McDonnell was invited to chair the first meetings. The Suttons and the Wexford gentry family of Talbot were intermarried. The first James Power, who founded Power's distillery, was repeating an established pattern of progression from Wexford to Dublin, and the marriage of his son to a daughter of J. H. Talbot of Castle Talbot in Co. Wexford, a family allied to the Suttons, made his business the continuation of a tradition that ran back as far as Thomas Sutton and his many family and business ties.

Thus Catholics, Quakers and other Dissenters were prominent in trade. Their number can be exaggerated, but the very fact that they were a minority gave them an advantage. Sons had to go far afield in search of success, and if they did well, the links they created could support relatives who stayed at home. Hence the success of the world of the Byrnes, McCarthys and Suttons. Dissenters were in the same position. The Dublin Quakers represented the business interests of co-religionists in the midlands and in Cork, while the city's Presbyterians enjoyed close ties with the linen districts of the north. Dissenters were a small proportion of the total Protestant freemen voters of Dublin in 1749 — some 17 percent in all, but they were disproportionately represented among the merchants, the richest category among the freemen, accounting for 107 of the 487 freemen merchant voters (22 percent). As minority groups Catholics and Dissenters also had a spirit of close cooperation, and could count on the backing of fellow-religionists. Thus when the manufacturing house of Comerford & O'Brien collapsed at the end of 1792 a Dublin Dissenter reported 'a dreadful earthquake in the mercantile world, failure of Comerford and O'Brien in the cotton line. Byrne etc. with other Catholics, for they are of that persuasion, offered £30,000 to O'Brien, but it was considered that it would not prove a stay'. It is not surprising that of the handful of really rich merchants the majority were Catholic or Dissenter, and that because they were successful, Catholics and Dissenters seemed more numerous in the wholesale trade of the city than they actually were.

James Power, founder of Power's whiskey distillery at John's Lane, Dublin in 1791.

The majority of the city's merchants belonged, in fact to the established church and in the aggregate handled a much larger volume of business than the others, even if overshadowed by the handful of powerful Quakers and Catholics. To some extent, even merchants belonging to the established church themselves felt discriminated against by the landed classes, and shared the radicalism of Quakers or Catholics. As a result, they were prominent even if not the driving force on the Committee of Merchants which was established in 1761, and hostility against the political establishment was very evident among the hard-pressed Protestant textile manufacturers of the Liberties in the 1790s.

There was however a prominent group among them which did business with the establishment, had many family ties with it and stood aside from the more radical and on the whole less wealthy merchant members of their own religion. Some of these merchants moved in the world of finance and banking. The La Touches are one of the most apposite examples. One of the family, James Digges La Touche, the only one who remained a merchant, was actively identified with the radical politics of the city in the 1740s. However, over the second half of the century the family steadily distanced itself from radical politics in the interests of its increasingly aristocratic business. Still on the opposition side in the 1770s, those members of the family who sat in the Irish House of Commons in subsequent decades were identified with government. Colebrooke's general business was represented in Dublin by one of the Sneyds, a family with close ties with the political establishment and the Church of Ireland. The wine trade was the most conservative of the major branches of the

city's trade. Customers were mainly among the landed classes and the wine merchants were conspicuously absent from the radical politics of the Committee of Merchants and even from the social milieu of the business world. The Bartons were destined to become one of the two largest merchant houses in Bordeaux in the 1770s. The eldest son, William, had been sent back to Ireland in the 1750s to a landed estate purchased in Co. Tipperary. William's cousin (another William) was a merchant in Dublin, and a pattern emerged, which lasted in the family, of combining the life of a landlowner in Ireland and trade either in Dublin or Bordeaux. The Sneyds retained an interest in the wine trade, and their business involvement was in time reflected in a member of the family becoming a director of the Bank of Ireland in 1799. In the early nineteenth century the greatest of all Irish wine houses, that of Barton, French & Sneyd, was formed by the Bartons and Sneyds with the Frenches of Co. Roscommon. All three had close political as well as social connections with the Irish landed establishment, and the house represented the apotheosis of conservative dealing in trade. The 1790s were also a period of renewed and aggressive involvement in banking by landed families and represented an assertive presence in Irish business by powerful families. It is not at all surprising that the Irish merchant community which enjoyed a good deal of common intercourse in earlier decades was deeply polarised in the 1790s, and that a deep and increasingly embittered gulf was reflected even in the history of the Chamber of Commerce.

Merchants represented the pinnacle of business life, which they dominated in the eighteenth century. Manufacturing was largely in the hands of small operators whose products ended up both for the home and foreign markets in the warehouses of merchants, just as the manufacturers acquired their raw materials by purchase from wholesalers rather than by import on their own account. Only those manufacturers who engaged in foreign trade by importing on their own account were the social equals of merchants, and they achieved this by being accepted as merchants in their own right rather than by their importance as manufacturers. Thus manufacturers in the worsted trade, because they did not wholesale worsted yarn in addition to processing it, seem to have been distinctly inferior to otherwise broadly similar manufacturers in cotton who were also wholesalers of the raw materials. If manufacture was looked down on, retail trade was very lowly except in wine where the customers conferred prestige on the product. The lifestyle of Dublin merchants was set out in one of the petitions of the Chamber of Commerce in 1787 about times for the post:

> From the established mode of transacting business in Dublin (not as in London through the medium of brokers) the merchant's entire morning must be devoted to the attendance on public markets in the sale or purchase of goods, executing the orders he receives by the post of the day, effecting insurances and to his other necessary avocations so as to render it impractical for him to sit down to business at home until the evening when by the present rule of the post he has not more than two or three hours for the arranging of his affairs and writing his letters which is evidently too short a space of time for the most trifling mercantile correspondence.

II

The Ouzel Galley Society
1705*1888

The complex relations between merchants in the city as well as the presence among them of a powerful caste were reflected in the character and history of the Ouzel Galley Society, an institution which also has an interest in its own right. It was in fact something of an unique institution, being at one and the same time a commercial arbitration body and a prestigious dining club. It had arisen originally out of the dilemmas posed by a vessel under Captain Massey, dispatched by the Dublin house of Ferris, Twigg and Cash to the Levant in 1695. The year 1695 was a year of war, made doubly dangerous in the case of vessels bound to the Levant by the activities of Algerine pirates who preyed on commercial traffic passing into and out of the Mediterranean. The full story of the adventures of the *Ouzel Galley* is obscure, although because of the celebrity of the issues raised by its unexpected return to home waters a number of rather fanciful accounts have been written about it. But adventurous its voyage must have been, because after the vessel had long been given up for lost, it reappeared in Dublin Bay in 1700, having taken about four times the normal time for a return voyage to the Levant. This, though highly unusual, would not in itself have sufficed for the vessel to acquire a niche in history. The underwriters had already paid out the insurance on the hull and cargo. But to whom did the return cargo belong? It did not belong to the owners because they had been fully compensated for their loss by the underwriters after the owners had made a formal act of abandoning their interest to them; but at the same time its return cargo did not belong to the underwriters because the abandon to them covered the vessel and its outward cargo, not the return cargo with which the vessel was laden on its unexpected reappearance. While existing practices covered normal situations and made possible the amicable settlement of most contracts, all the uncertainties in marine assurance were to the fore in this unusual situation. An action in law started in 1700. Litigation was notoriously slow and expensive, and the prospects of a speedy resolution seemed even less likely in a case involving issues as complex and unusual as the *Ouzel Galley* presented.

Wisely, the issue was settled in 1705 by the submission of the matter to the arbitration of a number of merchants. From this instance of arbitration in an isolated and complex case arose the Ouzel Galley Society as a permanent arbitration body of merchants. Eighteenth-century merchants everywhere in western Europe quite frequently submitted complex matters to the arbitration of fellow merchants by private arrangement. The significance of the Ouzel Galley Society lay in the systematisation of arbitration by prominent

merchants who were widely respected for their standing into a permanent private tribunal to which both parties to a commercial dispute could have recourse if they agreed. The attraction of such arbitration proceedings for merchants was that many disputes hinged less on fine points of law than on issues which could be more readily decided by practical knowledge of commodities and accepted practices. For instance, the condition of goods was one frequent source of disagreement among merchants, while another source of contention was whether one party to a transaction had departed from what could be regarded as the common code of practice and whose observance the other party would have taken for granted. The law courts themselves would have had to resort to merchants for an opinion on matters such as the condition of goods or the practices in trade, and it was therefore only common sense to seek the arbitration of merchants whose standing would have made them the decisive witnesses in court proceedings.

Little is known about the early activities of the Society as records were lost on several occasions in its history. But its purpose as set out in 1799, when its practices were codified and revised, probably accurately reflect its original objectives:

> It is the duty of all Members of the Galley to sit as arbitrators in the settlement of any matter in dispute to them referred, provided all the Arbitrators chosen are Members of the Galley.

> Parties are not to make any personal application whatsoever to Members of the Galley, either respecting their appointment as Arbitrators, or the subject of the matter in dispute. Respecting the appointment, the parties, after they have chosen Arbitrators, are to acquaint the Registrar, whose duty it is to inform the Members chosen; and respecting the matter in dispute, it must be spoken of before the Arbitrators, only in the presence of the parties or their agents; or where cases of evidence in writing are submitted, they must be transmitted, sealed up, through the hands of the Registrar.

> The parties referrring matters to arbitration are to deposit with the Registrar a sum of money to insure the payment of the Galley Fees, which are appropriated, after the payment of the costs of the award, to a charitable fund.

Ouzel Galley Society medals by Isaac Parkes, c.1850. The Ouzel Galley Goblet.

Parties to have the choice of their Arbitrators; but the Arbitrators, in all cases, to have the appointment of an Umpire, if necessary.

The Society was confined to a maximum of 40 members, i.e. a number corresponding to the size of the crew of the *Ouzel Galley*. Its officers were denominated as the Captain, two Lieutenants, Master, Bursar, Boatswain, Gunner, Carpenter, Master's Mate, Coxwain, Boatswain's Mate, Gunner's Mate, and Carpenter's Mate. The Captain, Lieutenants, Master, Bursar, Boatswain, Gunner and Carpenter formed the Council. The other members were known as the hands. Such a crew would have corresponded to the crew of a sizeable merchantman, armed and carrying in war-time a large number of men to provide for the defence as well as navigation of the vessel. From 1760 the rules clearly provided for a ballot, and a new member required a majority of two-thirds of the officers and hands present at a meeting. By the 1740s the Society seems to have lost ground: the election of 15 members on 12 June 1751 would suggest that its membership had been allowed to fall and that it was not an eagerly sought privilege. Moreover, the fact that the pre-1753 records were noted as having been missing at the time of codifying the Society's practices in 1799 may offer something of a commentary on its efficiency in the years just before the early 1750s. The revival of the Society's fortunes and more certainly its acquisition of social prestige seems to have been due to John Macarell, a merchant, banker and city alderman who also served as Lord Mayor. He became captain in 1748, and the evidence of vigour follows closely on his election: the election of 15 new members in 1751 and the survival continuously from 1753 (at least until 1799) of records of the Society. In 1753 Macarell commissioned a large painting of the *Ouzel Galley* which was put on display in the Ship Tavern in Chapelizod where the Society dined at that time. The innkeeper, John Morris, gave his receipt to the Society, dated 1 August 1753:

> Received from John Macarell Esqr., Captain of the *Ouzel Galley* a large painted piece representing the *Ouzel Galley* which is put up in the great room in my house. And I do hereby acknowledge that the said painted piece is the property of the said Galley, and that I will deliver the said when demanded by the said Captain Macarell, or to the majority of the Crew belonging to the said Galley.

27

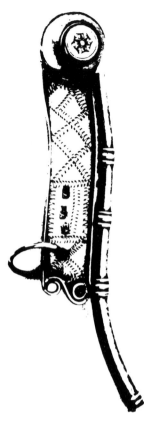

The Boatswain's whistle, c.1770.

The painting was later to pass out of the possession of the Society and many years were to elapse before it was recovered to stand as it has since 1870 in the council chamber of the Chamber of Commerce. Whether the Society was already a dining club is not quite clear, and it is possible that John Macarell gave an impetus to what appears to have been a flagging institution by turning it into a dining club: his commissioning of the painting and its location in a tavern may suggest as much. The titles bestowed on the officers, their large number, the evidence of ritual (e.g. such as a silver whistle for the boatswain), reveal too something of the passion for ceremony and "belonging" characteristic of the age and satisfied not only by Freemasonry but by the Hell-fire clubs and so on which, whatever the later legends which have grown up around them, were harmless enough in their day.

Even in its decay in the 1740s the membership of the Society, as one would expect of a body whose members had to command the respect which would lead to their acceptance by both parties in commercial disputes, was very exclusive. Macarell was able to enhance this standing further and also to give it a decidedly conservative flavour. He belonged to a clique with whom the city guilds, including the Guild of Merchants, were at loggerheads, and Macarell became captain in fact at a time when the conflict between the Aldermen and the more democratic Common Council of the Corporation was at its height. He was also a partner in a bank which was closely identified with the landed classes. Aldermen were well represented among the Society's members, and the conservative and exclusive stamp of membership is evident also in the prominent place of the city's wine merchants in the Society. Macarell was himself a wine merchant. William Delap, father of Samuel Delap of Bordeaux who was a partner of Thomas Barton also of Bordeaux, was already a member in 1748. Thomas Barton of Bordeaux was himself one of the fifteen members elected in 1751, and William Barton (it is not clear whether the son or the Dublin relative of Thomas, both bearing the name William), was elected in 1762. Albert Gledstanes, long in the wine trade and whose son was to emigrate and settle in Bordeaux as a merchant, was elected in 1756. No less than four of the members of the early fifties had associations with the banking world of the day. Thus, the Galley was dominated in that decade by a powerful and interconnected group of aldermen, wine merchants and bankers.

Conservative though the Ouzel Galley was, its membership changed after 1756. In fact, over the succeeding eighty years or so the Society was to reflect rather sensitively the prevailing outlook of the merchant aristocracy of the city. Extremely exclusive in the 1750s, it was to become liberal or radical between the 1750s and the 1790s, to revert under the strains of the revolutionary decade of the 1790s to a conservative and exclusive stance. In 1756 this conservative and large Anglican group elected the Quaker John Pim Joshua and in 1757 it elected another Quaker, the banker Joseph Fade. On this in all probability hangs a tale. Fade had been one of the founders of the bank of Willcocks & Dawson which had failed in 1755. The onslaught on the business world that the banking act in 1756 implied helped to ensure a degree of common ground in the following years between Quaker and Dissenter merchants and those merchants who belonged to the established church. The underlying caution and conservativeness of the Galley is evident however in the fact that, though Catholics were to play a prominent role in the Committee of Merchants which was founded in 1761, they were slow to be elected to the Ouzel Galley. Anthony McDermott, wealthy merchant and prominent figure in the Committee of Merchants though he was, was elected only in 1783, the year in which he died, and no further Catholic was elected until Valentine O'Connor in 1791, D. Thomas O'Brien in 1796 and Randal McDonnell in 1800.

However, even if the Ouzel Galley drew the line at Catholics, there is no doubting the liberal stance evident from the end of the 1750s. In the 1760s, a period when the sensitivities of merchants were increasingly heightened on the political front and when political reform was becoming the objective of a small but growing "Patriot" group of landed gentry in parliament, the radical element in the Ouzel Galley increased significantly. The dissenter Travers Hartley was elected in 1762 and the Quaker Hosea Coates in 1763. A further three Quakers were to be elected in subsequent years: Joseph Pike in 1768, Edward Strettell in 1769 and Joshua Pim in 1776. Of 42 members elected between 1762 and 1783 no less than 19 were or became members of the Committee of Merchants. In the years 1778-1782 in particular, when the momentous questions of free trade and a free parliament were the political issues of the day, a number of rich but radical members were admitted, and the first Catholic appeared in 1783. On 16 April 1782 the Ouzel Galley passed a resolution:

> RESOLVED — That the King, Lords and Commons of Ireland are solely competent to make laws for the Government thereof and that we will pay obedience to such laws only as have received or shall receive their sanctions.
> RESOLVED — That the Captain, Officers and Crew of this Galley cooperate with their country-men in every constitutional effort to support the just rights of Ireland and to oppose the interference of any other legislature.

Radical members continued to be elected in the 1780s, such as the brother of Travers Hartley in 1784 and William Cope in 1786. No less a figure than Travers Hartley himself became Captain in 1791, a measure of the hold of radical opinion on merchants at all levels at that time.

The continued election of members of the La Touche family, though no longer involved in trade (three between 1776 and 1798) or of Robert Shaw in 1788 illustrates however how the Galley even at this stage was an uneasy alliance of what were at heart virtually incompatible interests. Its composition became more conservative as the Revolution discredited radicals, and this trend was particularly evident in the election of Arthur Guinness in 1804 and Nathaniel Sneyd in 1809. The Pims were the only Quaker family to feature in its nineteenth-century membership and after 1800 no new Catholic member appeared —at least before 1821. Most of the Catholics elected appear from 1830 onwards when the anti-Popery clause was dropped in the wake of Catholic Emancipation from the oath administered to directors of the Bank of Ireland, and they were drawn from the handful of Catholic families prominent in financial circles. William Dargan did appear in 1853, but his election reflected his organisation of the Dublin

William Dargan, born Co. Carlow, 1799, died Dublin 1867. Railway contractor and moving spirit behind the great Dublin Exhibition of 1853. The National Gallery, Merrion Square, was built to commemorate his services, and his statue stands in front of it.

exhibition of that year rather than an accepted place in the Dublin merchant world.

Increasingly in the early decades of the nineteenth century, the Ouzel Galley reverted to being a narrow body associated with families prominent in the financial life of the city or after the mid-twenties with the very narrow circle who finally came to dominate the Chamber of Commerce. The 1830s and 1840s were in fact, the last period in which the Ouzel Galley was really active. Subsequently, its decline became evident and accelerated as time passed. Members were not replaced; meetings and dinners did not take place. Its last dinner was held in 1880, and the Society was wound up in 1888. Its decline as a commercial arbitration body preceded its social decline. While 318 awards were made between 1799 and 1869, the bulk were made before 1824. From that date the Society's importance in arbitration proceedings began to fall away: there was not a single award in 1836.

Throughout its history, at least until the 1820s, the Society had played a useful role in arbitration in mercantile matters. While its social role had increased from the 1750s, it gave the Ouzel Galley an importance in cementing together the group who dominated the Committee of Merchants and the Chamber of Commerce which in 1783 replaced the

Committee. The radicals of the day were as tightly-knit as the conservatives. As we can perceive from the patterns of membership of Galley as well as Committee and Chamber, the three bodies reinforced each other from the 1760s into the 1790s. These were the decades when the influence of the Ouzel Galley was at its peak, reaching beyond arbitration and social activity even into the political field. Moreover, while the Galley in these years remained exclusive in its membership, its increasingly radical composition minimised the gulf between it and the wider merchant constituency represented by the Committee and the Chamber. The radical departure of the Ouzel Galley from the late 1750s or early 1760s represented something of a dramatic shift for what was a small and exclusive body. Indeed such a body could hardly change in such a fashion from any internal momentum, and it required the impetus to change given by great external forces both to involve such a body in wider issues and to transform its own outlook. Dublin was in a ferment in the 1760s and 1770s. Its trade was growing rapidly, and the size and interests of its merchant community were also expanding in response to the commercial opportunities of the day. Politically, too, life was changing rapidly in these decades, and for a strengthened and enlarged merchant community political issues, formerly the prerogative of the country's landed gentlemen who gathered in parliament every second autumn, had acquired for the first time a real relevance. It is worth considering both these interacting forces: the growth of Dublin business and the political tensions of the era.

The 1760s represented a fertile period in the growth of Dublin business. The linen trade grew with remarkable rapidity in that decade: so too did the worsted yarn trade which was the basis of the wealth and position of both John Pim and Abraham Wilkinson. Two staples of the continental trade reached their peak at the end of the decade: beef outwards, and wine inwards. Brandy, usually a relative minor trade, also took on a major importance between 1756 and 1767 as first war led it to replace rum and later poor harvests to replace whiskey. Laurence Saule decided to leave Dublin for Cognac in 1759 ostensibly for religious reasons, but James Delamain of Huguenot ancestry left as well. For a decade from 1757, the Dublin market was the main business of the Cognac region, and the Irish houses which settled there in that decade played a crucial role in the rise of the modern brandy trade. Within Dublin, the rapid growth of trade gave an impetus to speculative forces. Colebrooke's interest in Dublin harnessed Irish capital to even wider speculative urges in London, attracting capital both from the Protestant financial circle around the Sneyds and a Catholic one around the Jennings and the other Dublin connections of the Saules. These were the years too in which Edward Byrne began his rise and at the end of the period Thomas Sutton began to build up his complex series of marriage alliances. A rapid growth in trade always led to new faces and new houses, and Dublin's commerce in the 1760s and early 1770s widened in the diversity of its backing, Catholics in particular beginning to become more numerous. The brandy trade, a highly speculative one in which a small investment seemed to offer a large reward, attracted many new faces, and helped to account for the sometimes precarious appearance of new houses. The contrasts in religions in trade provided a fascinating pattern of social mobility. Anglicans dominated long-established branches of trade, and especially the lucrative

Commemorative stamp issued on February 23, 1983, showing the Ouzel Galley Goblet.

wine trade; Quakers and Dissenters on the other hand, controlling the sources of supply in the midlands and in Ulster, monopolised the new-found importance of textiles in mid-century. Brandy, whose importance was a feature of the 1750s and 1760s was almost as Catholic as wine was Protestant: Anthony McDermott the elder was a central figure in the brandy business.

If the 1760s were significant because of their economic forces, they were important also because of underlying political tensions. The powerful parliamentary group which overawed the executive in the Castle in the 1750s was unpopular in the city. The riots by mobs from the Protestant liberties before the Houses of Parliament in 1759 illustrated the depth of this unpopularity which reached far down the social scale. Riots were not countenanced by the better off, but even they had their own reasons to resent the arrogance of the landed classes in parliament. Within parliament itself a small but growing body of patriot members, seeking reform, represented a challenge to the three or four compact groups of political grandees or "undertakers" who dominated parliamentary and political life. The merchants were long to have close relations with the radical or patriot members of parliament. A few radical merchants themselves were to sit in parliament like William Colvill who purchased a seat in 1777 or more significantly, because he was elected at the hustings for the city of Dublin in 1782, Travers Hartley. The patriot members were free from the popular opprobrium that attached to parliament as a whole, and sitting in the main for constituencies in and around Dublin, they also reflected an arresting rift between on the one hand the capital allied to the landed families of its vicinity and on the other hand the powerful rural groups of Boyles from Cork, Gores from the northwest, and Clements from the north midlands who represented the landed classes undiluted by any material interests in the capital. Significantly, the greatest of the "undertaker" groups, the Boyles, not directly involved in the Dublin financial world, did not sit on the Wide Street Commissioners, while the other groups were directly represented among them.

Resentment experienced by the businessmen in the Liberties and city as well as expressed violently by the lower orders provided ground for novel common cause between Protestant, Quaker and Catholic merchants. Common cause in turn implied concerted action against the source of complaint, and a new and novel assertiveness. Everywhere indeed the 1760s were a decade of assertiveness, ranging from peasant agrarian movements in Ulster and Munster to the organised activity of Catholics and merchants in pursuit of their own interests. Catholics in 1759 founded a Catholic Committee which began to campaign cautiously for a repeal of some of the restrictions affecting them. The Committee of Merchants, founded almost contemporaneously in 1761, was a body established by another disadvantaged group. The foreign trade of the country was never again to show signs of promise in so many directions simultaneously: these were to be the years in which merchants found a sense of confidence fed by their growing wealth. Merchants, many of them members of the Guild of Merchants or of the Common Council of the Corporation, had absorbed the language of democracy as well, and the links between politics in the city of Dublin and the patriot group in parliament were bound also to determine the political terms in which they viewed the world around them. An interacting circle of growing economic wealth, political resentment, and a new-found spirit of assertiveness explained both the origins and character of the Committee of Merchants. Out of it too, at a later date, grew the Chamber of Commerce, consisting largely of the same men and motivated by the same spirit as the Committee.

III

The Committee of Merchants
1761*1783

Merchants were, for the reasons set out in the preceding chapter, a comparatively radical group in the 1760s. In the north the disenchantment of Presbyterians with the landed classes and with the Dublin parliament was beginning to become evident, and even the Catholics, still suffering under the penal laws, orchestrated in the course of the 1760s a case for relief. Merchants could hardly avoid the feeling of resentment around them. Economic growth was making them wealthy, and the fact that many of them were members of the established church meant that they were freer than either Catholics or Presbyterians to be assertive. They were drawn towards the small but growing number of Protestants who laid an emphasis on parliamentary reform and who provided the nucleus of the patriot group in the Irish parliament. This group itself, like so many of the aspects of Irish life was subservient, to the "undertakers" or political grandees, but when a strong resident Lord Lieutenant, Townshend, took on the dominant politicians between 1767 and 1772 and defeated them, it was able to become a more central force in political life. The representation for Dublin city in the Irish parliament was already on the side of reform, and the majority of the members returned in the adjoining counties both for the county and boroughs were on the same side. In particular the Earl of Kildare and the relatives and retainers which his influence was able to get elected in Kildare and in Meath were arraigned on the side of the patriots. The 'Leinster' block in the Commons was thus allied to the city representation which in the 1760s consisted of a member of the Fitzgerald (or Leinster) family and Charles Lucas. Lucas had been involved in a violent conflict with the administration in the late 1740s and had only come back from exile to be elected in 1761. In the stormy Dublin election of 1749 one of his supporters had been Thomas Read who featured in the membership of the Committee of Merchants established in 1761. Dublin local politics were all the more bitter because they represented a conflict between the Common Council of the Corporation on which the guilds, including the Guild of Merchants, was represented and a self-perpetuating oligarchy who comprised the Board of Aldermen. It is not surprising, therefore, that in the 1760s the merchants displayed some hostility to parliament and had a complex relationship with the municipality marked by many ties with the guilds and Common Council and at the same time a dislike of the charges which the municipality imposed on the merchant community either through taxes or the officers who supervised or regulated trade.

The Case of the Merchants of Dublin, the first public statement of their position by the Committee in 1768, displayed a good deal of antipathy for the Corporation:

> The merchants of the city of Dublin (having had long experience of the utter inattention of corporate bodies to the interest of trade, although the original purpose of their institution; and observing the generality of them entirely taken up in contests for little distinctions of pre-eminence among themselves and eagerly engaged in the pursuit of the honours or emoluments of magistracy) formed themselves in the year 1761 into a voluntary society, composed indiscriminately of all merchants who are willing to join in defraying the necessary expence of such an institution, the mere objects of which were the defence of trade against any illegal imposition, and the solicitation of such laws as might prove beneficial to it.

The composition of the Committee is interesting because it drew some of its support from merchants such as Travers Hartley and Thomas Read, deeply involved in the politics of the Corporation. Hartley, who was the most prominent member of the Committee and who was to become the first president of its successor body the Chamber of Commerce, had much influence in the guilds and was a member of Parliament for the city from 1782 to 1790. After his election in 1782 he was described as 'a dissenter — a merchant of eminence, knowledge and integrity — . . . will obey any instructions his constituents shall think proper to give'. The nucleus of the Committee consisted of prominent Dublin merchants, some of them members of the Church of Ireland. Some significant merchants, however, did not become involved: names such as Gledstanes, Barton, Sneyd or Arthur Guinness, very prominent in the life of the city, do not feature on the Committee. Nor did the name of Jeremiah Vickers, who in 1783 was the only merchant to subscribe the maximum permissible investment of £10,000 at the launching of the Bank of Ireland. Wealth was not however the criterion which distinguished such merchants; the Committee represented most of the rich merchants, and the distinction would seem to lie more in the existence of ties with the landed classes. For instance, William Barton was already establishing himself as a landed gentleman in Co. Tipperary, had married into the staunchly establishment family of Massy in Co. Limerick and controlled half the political interest of the borough of Fethard in Co. Tipperary.

The Committee is particularly interesting because of the fact that no less than six of its 21-man committee were either Catholic or Quaker. The two Quakers were John Pim Joshua, one of Dublin's most powerful merchants who was to move to London around 1770 and whose successor on the Committee, Joshua Pim, was one of the progenitors of the 1783 proposal for a Chamber of Commerce; and Edward Strettell, from a family long identified with trade in the city. Strettell was replaced on his decease in 1781 by another Quaker, Joshua Clibborn. There were already four Catholics on the Committee in the 1760s, Anthony and Owen McDermott, Michael Cosgrave and John Connor. A fifth, Thomas Broughall, was elected in 1771, and when John Connor died in 1772 he was replaced by Denis Thomas O'Brien as 'a proper person to fill up said vacancy'. *The Case of the Merchants of Dublin* in 1768 laid a heavy emphasis on the fact that "the choice of that Committee

has been made on the same liberal principles on which the Society was originally formed, no regard being had in it, to any difference of party or opinion, but merely to consideration in trade or capacity, and active disposition to be useful". Quaker or Catholic members presided over meetings just as readily as other merchants; at one meeting in 1772, no less than four of the six members present were Catholic, and in the 1770s Anthony McDermott was appointed one of the three trustees for the funds for the new Royal Exchange.

The Catholic members of the Committee of Merchants, it should be noted, were also among the active members of the Catholic Committee, and in 1779 a letter from Lords Gormanston and Kenmare informed the Catholic prelates that Anthony McDermott, 'a gentleman whose worth and integrity you can not be a stranger to', had been appointed treasurer of the Catholic Committee. In 1783, McDermott's subscription of £8,000 was next to Vickers', the largest mercantile investment in the Bank of Ireland

The fact that a third of the Committee were either Quaker or Catholic is quite remarkable in the temper of the times especially as this grossly overrated the relative weight of Catholic or Quaker wealth in the city's business community. Moreover, this does not include other Dissenters, of whom there were at least two (Travers Hartley and Robert Black) — and certainly more — on the Committee, or merchants like Alexander and Robert Jaffray and Abraham Wilkinson who came from a Quaker milieu but do not appear themselves to have been Quakers. In consequence the Committee was very unrepresentative of the bulk of the city's businessmen and wealth, itself a factor which gave it a radical image which can hardly have recommended it to the conservative members of parliament or indeed to the more conservative of fellow merchants.

It is sometimes assumed that the Committee had been formed for the purpose of resisting the efforts of Thomas Allan, appointed to the sinecure of wine taster in 1763, to revive old impositions; but this is a misunderstanding which arises simply because the early minute book does not survive, and the first page of the first surviving minute book records a decision in 1767 to retain counsel to challenge Allan's demands. In fact, it was opposition, not to Allan but to municipal demands which seems to have been the original reason for the foundation of the Committee, which occupied itself from time to time with a varied range of mercantile preoccupations. One of the costs in a bill from counsel in 1767 included an item from July 1765 in respect of 'drawing up an Association of the merchants in the beef trade in opposition to the slaughtering butchers . . .'. Industrial trouble was again on the agenda in 1769 when the Committee sent a memorial to the Lord Lieutenant regarding a combination among journeymen coopers, and it provided £50 to the Corporation of Coopers in order to defray the costs of prosecuting the offending journeymen. Its strong support from the powerful Quaker interest in the worsted yarn trade helps to explain why the Committee decided on 10 March 1773 to call a general meeting of merchants at the Guildhall to consider a violent attack by a mob on a cargo of worsted yarn for export from Dublin, noting that 'yarn furnishes the principal employment and support to the poor of several counties in this kingdom'. The reason behind the attack was the resentment of underemployed woollen workers against the export of worsted yarn which could be worked up into cloth in the city. At this time, competition among the exporters of worsted yarn from the major ports was acute, since the supply was contracting as tillage encroached on traditional pasturage. The Committee noted the danger that if such outrages took place, the trade in yarn would simply shift to other ports free from the danger of attack.

As far back as 1769 the Committee was in touch with the merchants of Cork and Belfast. It also interested itself in wider economic issues. In December 1769, after taking into account 'the present declining state of public credit', it formulated a resolution to support the banks of La Touche, Gleadowe, Finlay and Coates & Lawless. The bank of Colebrooke had actually deferred payment of its notes, and the Committee was anxious to forestall a wider crisis. The Committee frequently addressed memorials to the Lord Lieutenant or sent deputations. This was quite novel at the time, and represented in political terms an informal alliance with the Lord Lieutenant over the head of parliament. In December 1770 and February 1771 it made representations to the Lord Lieutenant regarding the embargo which had been imposed on the provisions trade because of the danger of the Falklands crisis leading to war. In February 1776 it summoned a general meeting of merchants as fresh embargoes reflected the fear of approaching war with France. In January 1770 Anthony McDermott, at the request of Sir Lucius O'Brien, put before the Committee the heads of a bill for creating a navigation from Dublin to the Shannon. This approach was followed later — in April 1773 — by a meeting between the undertakers of the Grand Canal Company, which arose from this legislation, and the Committee. The involvement of the merchants in the project was sought, but the Committee decided to remain unconnected. This denotes a rather marked caution. It should be noted — significantly as the Committee had been approached through Anthony McDermott — that many of the city's Catholic merchants including McDermott himself invested in the project, as did some other merchants including the Pims. If the merchants had been involved more centrally it might not have become landlord-dominated as proved to be the case in the 1780s, and the Royal Canal scheme might never have taken shape as it did a a rather forlorn opposition venture directed against the political establishment.

Although it had not been the reason for the establishment of the Committee, the building of the Royal Exchange was its main continuing task in the 1760s and 1770s, and helps to explain why the Committee functioned well in these two decades in contrast to the poor and intermittent success of organisations among Dublin merchants in the subsequent thirty years. The task was an expression of the self-confidence of the merchants who repeatedly pointed to the want of a proper exchange building in Dublin. Symbolically, too, the proposal represented a gesture of independence in regard to the disliked corporation of the city. The Committee had since its institution met in the Tholsel. *The Memorial of the Merchants of Dublin* in 1768 painted a picture of 'their meeting at the Tholsel, where the city courts are held, which occasion a frequent concourse of the meanest and most licentious of the people, while from beneath issue the steams of kitchens reeking with preparations of city entertainments . . .'. The acquisition of land by the new Wide Street Commissioners for the purpose of creating the modern Parliament Street provided the occasion for the proposal to build the Exchange. In November 1765 a petition of the merchants of Dublin,

The Tholsel (1683), Skinner Row, by James Malton.

38

supported by the Committee, asked parliament to reserve a site for an exchange building which it would erect at its own expense. In February 1766 a committee of the commons supported the proposal, and eventually it provided the funds for the acquisition of the site by the Wide Street Commissioners. In 1766 the Committee started the series of lotteries which were intended to raise the funds to defray the costs of the project. The sequence of events illustrates how wrong is the suggestion that the conclusion of the Allan case when a surplus of money was left in the hands of the merchants led them to decide on an exchange. The Allan case was not decided till 1768 while the exchange idea was mooted by the merchants in a petition to Parliament as early as three years previously. By October 1767 the committee was able confidently to minute that 'the exchange scheme for this present year is so far advanced as to prevent any doubt of its success', and in November 1767 it nominated sixteen trustees in whom the ground would be vested. In approaching parliament directly, significantly it had bypassed the Corporation, which counterattacked before legislation for the exchange had actually had the approval of parliament. In 1768 the Corporation determined to petition for permission to erect an exchange building of its own. The Committee of Merchants decided on 26 January 1768 that they could not accept this, and resolved to proceed with its own plans. At this meeting the draft of *The Case of the Merchants of the City of Dublin* was produced, apparently written by Travers Hartley, and shortly afterwards counsel were retained to plead the Committee's case at the bar of the House of Commons. The Committee decided that the site should be conveyed to the Guild of Merchants, and that the planning of the building be entrusted to a Committee consisting of the original trustees plus 15 merchants chosen by the wholesale members of the Guild. The Committee had retained counsel to draw up heads of a bill, and appointed an agent to look after their interests in London when it was considered by the Privy Council. The bill as passed by Parliament largely met their case. The act in effect turned down the Corporation's proposal; it created a body consisting of named members of the Committee of Merchants and senior members of the Guild of Merchants. Any deceased members would be replaced by elections by the Guild of Merchants, but only by its wholesale members. Land for the site was still being acquired at the end of the 1760s, but in February 1774 the new building was reported to be 'nearly completed'. In all, 14 lotteries from 1766 to 1779 raised a gross total of £86,931, leaving a net amount of £49,441.

In mooting an ambitious and expensive Royal Exchange, the members of the Committee had assumed a stable world around them in which the only changes would be the new wide street (Parliament Street) and the exchange building at its head. However, though Dublin was populated mainly by merchants, artificers and others engaged in trade and industry, it was dominated socially by the landed classes, and by the Wide Street Commissioners, an offshoot of the Irish parliament which had as its aim the embellishment of the environment rather than the cultivation of the city's interests as merchants saw them. The Wide Street Commissioners consisted of the Lord Mayor (no friend of the merchants) and of twenty grandees appointed by Parliament. They were all landed magnates whose economic interests lay outside Dublin. Moreover, through John Ponsonby, Speaker of the Commons, Anthony Malone, Chancellor of the Exchequer, and Sir Arthur Gore, the dominant political interests in the Irish Commons also controlled the Commissioners. Not a single merchant sat on the Board; and as two of the Commissioners were also Commissioners of the Revenue the Wide Streets Commissioners and the Revenue Board were in the matter of the siting of a new custom house able to find common ground to the total dismay of the merchants. The fashionable areas in Dublin were to the east of the city: hence its superior inhabitants were well aware of its noise, smells and fumes. Quite apart from the Wide Street Commissioners, which were a sweeping expression of Parliament's sovereign power over the city, other legislation from the middle of the century also regulated or removed from the city several noisome industries. Even more arrogantly, in 1756 at a time when the undertaker interest in the Irish parliament had won the political tussle with the executive, the bank act had actually prohibited merchants engaged in foreign trade from conducting a banking business.

All this legislation represented a situation in which parliament had its own views of circumstances around it, and arrogantly imposed its view on the city's community through legislation. Tension was built into this situation from the very moment when merchants, like the Catholics, were prepared to organise in furtherance of their interests. Merchants were bound to come into conflict with the dominant group in parliament which revolved around the great parliamentary families who controlled a phalanx of seats in the Commons held by retainers and relatives. *An address to the Committee of the Merchants' Society*, dated 22 October 1761, provides some evidence of the pressures to which the Committee was subject in the direction of confronting political grandees; this situation in fact justified the caution of which the author of the anonymous *Address* complained. The natural allies of the merchants were bound to be on the one hand the Lord Lieutenant and the officials around him who represented the royal authority now increasingly determined to break the power of the undertakers, and on the other hand the Patriot element in the House of Commons, the popular or reforming members who rightly identified the undertakers as a vested interest in parliament who stood against reform. Thus the merchants were well-disposed towards the Lord Lieutenant, and especially towards Townshend who was Lord Lieutenant from 1767 to 1772. Open conflict between the Lord Lieutenant and the undertakers broke out in the session that began in October 1769; two months previously in August the Committee had taken the unprecedented step for such a lowly body (for that was what a group of merchants were however rich its members), of entertaining the Lord Lieutenant to a lavish dinner in the Tholsel in 1769 at a cost of £299. On the other hand, they were the butt of the contempt of the politicians. When a deputation was received by the Revenue Commissioners in April 1769, they were treated with gross incivility by Bellingham Boyle, a member of the Boyle family who constituted the most powerful undertaker group in the Irish parliament. According to the minutes of 11 April 1769:

> Mr. Sutton further informed the Committee that Bellingham Boyle Esq., one of the commissioners entered the Room during the conversation and treated your sub-committee in so uncivil and rude a manner that they were under a necessity of retiring.

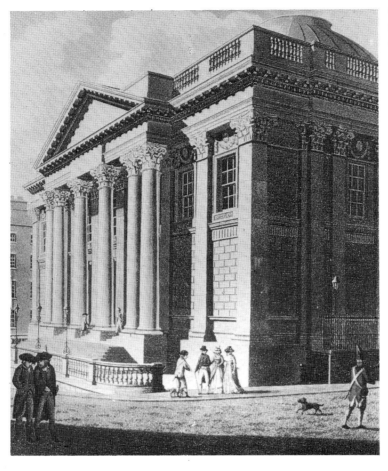

The occasion of this visit and of the resulting incivility was the emergence of the proposal from the Revenue Commissioners to build a new custom house further downstream from the existing one beside Essex Bridge, which was only a stone's throw from the site of the new Royal Exchange. The Commissioners consisted of politicians who were members or nominees of the undertakers, and this proposal appeared as a further arrogant instance of political insouciance about the interests of others. It was all the more disturbing because the merchants rightly feared, as events were to prove, that if the custom house were built further downstream this would result in the building of a new bridge which would isolate the old business centre of the city from the sea. The merchants were to remain opposed to the resiting of the custom house until the very end. One of the consequences was that the new building was denounced as it began to rise by liberal politicians, Grattan describing it in 1790 as 'of sixth-rate rank in architecture, but of first-rate extravagance'.

Merchants and gentry inhabited very different worlds. When the former petitioned the Lord Lieutenant on the subject of the custom house in 1774,

The new Custom House, James Gandon, architect. The foundation stone was laid on August 8, 1781. From an aquatint by James Malton.

the most revealing aspect of the petition was not the conflict of interest, real though it was, but the humble role and place in society in relation to the parliamentary classes which at least publicly the merchants accepted for themselves. The Committee represented that:

> Your petitioners are thoroughly convinced that no argument can be adduced in support of this measure which has any meaning in it, unless the convenience of the nobility and gentry, by affording them more direct and quick passage from and to the north-east and south-east quarters of the town. Your petitioners sincerely wish every accommodation to people of their rank, that could be obtained without so expensive a sacrifice of the navigation and trade of this city... They hope that those of their superiors who have solicited this measure, not from any private uninterested views, but merely from an idea of convenience, will cheerfully relinquish an accommodation of so little importance to them, rather than thus deeply injure the commercial interest of the metropolis.

As an argument against any change, they represented the danger of the merchants and their way of life invading the new districts:

Your petitioners beg leave further to observe, that, in consequence of building a bridge and custom house in the situation proposed all the hurry, crowd and annoyance which necessarily attend trade, will be brought even to the doors of our nobility and gentry, and many of those elegant streets in which they now reside, will become the common passages for porters and carts, loaded with the necessaries of life, and all kinds of merchandise, to be diffused throughout the whole city. Wherever the seat of trade is fixed, to that neighbourhood the merchants, with all their train, will in time remove themselves. The nobility and gentry are best secured against these inconveniences by continuing the custom house in its present situation.

A significant measure of the alienation of the Committee of Merchants from the grandees was their close collaboration with the legal officers of the crown in the 1760s and 1770s. They frequently retained them as counsel (crown officers were free to take private briefs at this time), and the attorney general on one occasion in 1767 even waived his fee; as the minutes read "the committee directed the agent to fee him handsomely but he would not take any fee, and gave his advice throughout". On 30 October 1767, at the same time as it decided to send a deputation to the Lord Lieutenant, it decided that 12 members of parliament should be waited on. They included the attorney general, solicitor general, prime serjeant, serjeant Dennis and Serjeant Lill, Anthony Malone, the greatest advocate of his day, two barrister members of Parliament, Morris and Lehunt, Perry and the three patriot figures of Flood, Dr Lucas and Sir Lucius O'Brien. Again in 1772 O'Brien, Malone, Flood, Hussey and the city members were consulted. The link with Anthony Malone, one of the most powerful figures in mid-eighteenth century Ireland but also the one about whom least is known, is intriguing. Malone, however, while an ally of Clements and the Gores (and like Clements married into the Gore family) had a Catholic background, and was alone among leading politicians in having some sympathy for Catholic relief. He was thus likely to have some understanding for the merchants' views, and in addition in the 1760s he seems to have shifted from a close identification with the undertakers to a broader political stance. It is significant too in the light of the banking act of 1756 that the Committee had no direct contact with the Dublin bankers now closely identified with the political establishment. The only exception was the banker John Dawson Coates with whom some continuing contact was maintained. He even attended a meeting in August 1774 when problems in the supply of guineas were discussed along with another man described as a banker who is unknown but who was probably a partner in Coates' house, William Dunn. He was present again at a Committee meeting in 1781. Parliament retained a dislike of the Committee, and even when it had become the Chamber of Commerce was pleased to take it down a peg. On 22 November 1783, when organised Dublin trade was at its peak with no less than 293 members in the Chamber, the House of Commons refused to accept 'the humble petition of the merchants comprising the Council of the Chamber of Commerce of the city of Dublin'. The Commons' objection was to the title of the petition, and the resubmitted petition in December had to avoid any claim of representing the city of Dublin at large. Much more humbly, they had to describe themselves merely as 'nominated a council by a numerous body of traders associated under the title of the Chamber of Commerce of the city of Dublin".

Merchants were still in a socially very ambiguous position. This is reflected in the very limited and cautious use of the epithet Esquire in the 1770s. It became much more general in the 1780s. The change coincided with a change in the style of names of Catholic merchants as well: for instance 'Mac' and 'O', which had often been dropped, were being brought back slowly, to become widespread in the 1780s. By 1783 the McDermotts were being recorded in the minutes of both the Chamber of Commerce and of the Catholic Committee with the Mac added to the Dermott, and were also identified as 'Esq'. But the equivocal usage of both 'Esq' and of 'O' and 'Mac' illustrates rather dramatically the social uncertainty of the merchants, as also a sense of insecurity which made them eager to adopt a new usage.

IV

'A general union among traders'
1783*1813

The Committee had now survived since 1761, meeting regularly, even if the number of meetings and the range of business items had tended to decline over the 1770s. But the renewed rumpus over the bridge in 1781 in combination with the heady democratic sentiments of 1782 and the prospects of free trade created a new impetus. Free trade had been conceded at the end of 1779; the new-found legislative independence of 1782 suggested that the Irish parliament could make trade arrangements of its own; and peace preliminaries in February 1783 held out to merchants the prospect of putting these advantages to effect as peace returned to the Atlantic world. A meeting of the Committee was held on 10 February 1783 'for the special purpose of taking into consideration a plan for instituting a Chamber of Commerce in this city'. The initiative for this proposal lay with John Patrick and Joshua Pim who presented to the Committee a plan for the institution of a Chamber of Commerce. A decision was taken by the Committee to resign as soon as 'the liberal and extensive' proposal was put into effect and the Council of the New Chamber had been elected. The plan was clearly inspired by the political events of the day:

> The present important situation of this country, its lately renewed constitution, its fond hopes of rising commerce and consequently increasing opulence, the variety of commercial regulations necessarily incident to this change of circumstance and particularly requisite from the late revolution in the political system: every consideration appearing to demand a general union among traders and a constant unwearied attention to their common interests; from a view whereof to promote these laudable objects in this particular district and to hold forth an example for imitation and cooperation to the rest of the kingdom.

It is likely too that it contained an unspoken sentiment of distrust of the ability of an unreformed parliament to look after the interests of merchants without a vigorous defence by them of their own concerns. The thrust of a formal organisation was to cement the alliance between the traders and the more radical members of parliament, who in opposition to the existing political establishment, sought reform. With an independent parliament secure, the line was sharply drawn between reforming members and those who wished to prevent the political revolution of 1782, which had made the Irish parliament constitutionally independent, from leading to wider reforms in political life. The support of the Council was to be thrown firmly on the side of the reformers.

Arthur Guinness, 1725-1803, founder of the Guinness brewery at St. James's Gate, 1759. Born at Celbridge, Co. Kildare, he is buried at Oughterard in the same county.

The paper from Patrick and Pim was short and to the point. It proposed a membership fee of one guinea and that 'any merchant or trader resident within the said city and its dependencies' would be eligible. Both men would act as temporary treasurers until a hundred subscriptions had been collected, at which stage a public meeting would be called to elect by ballot a council, which would be re-elected annually. That the initiative responded to the enthusiasm of the hour is shown by the success of the venture. The Council was elected on 18 March. Indeed the response exceeded expectations: the highest ballot received by any member at that meeting was 153, and in all 293 merchants paid subscriptions for 1783. The names of 219 of the subscribers survive in a contemporary broadsheet. While the great wine merchants were conspicuously absent, the members included many conservative merchants such as Jeremiah Vickers, Arthur Guinness, David Jebb, the 'great flour miller of Slane' who was a close friend of John Foster, one of the three most powerful members of the political establishment, and Robert Brooke, the greatest of the early landlord cotton manufacturers. Radicals were represented in force. Oliver Bond, the woollen draper, a future and ill-fated leader of the United Irishmen, was present, as was the most demagogic of all merchants and conspirators, James Napper Tandy. Two major decisions were taken at the public meeting in March. The first was to elect a Council of 41 members. The number had not been specified by Patrick and Pim in their plan, and this, though it made for an unwieldly committee, reflected the prevailing enthusiasm and democratic sentiments. The second decision was to appoint a full-time salaried secretary of the Chamber: William Shannon, appointed at a salary of £30 per annum. The former Committee had no full time staff, and had relied on the retained services of an attorney to do its secretarial work.

The liberal sentiments of the meeting were reflected also in the fact that at least six Catholics and one Quaker were elected to the Council. The Quaker and Catholic merchants received a relatively high number of ballots: the Quaker Pim and two members of Quaker background, Jaffray and Wilkinson, were in the first eight, and four Catholics in the first twenty (Valentine O'Connor, Denis Thomas O'Brien, Edward Byrne, Anthony McDermott). Most of the Protestant merchants elected were to remain attached to the radical cause through the 1780s and early 1790s. Indeed, the election had been dominated by radical ballots. Only a handful of the members of the Council can be identified either as conservatives at the time or as throwing in their lot in the 1780s with the political establishment. (It may even have been too radical and somewhat unrepresentative for its own survival.) The Council was in all probability from the start identified with the radicals. None of the prominent wine merchants were on it, for instance, and Vickers served only for one year, 1783. With the exception of Vickers, D'Olier and Brooke either few conservatives had offered themselves, or else the radical temper of the meeting did not admit of their election. The distribution of the ballots shows quite clearly that Dissenters, radicals and prominent Catholics polled best, and others much less well. Although it is not possible to piece together the full story, the assembly of merchants in March was clearly both radical and generous in its outlook. This was reflected too in the policy followed by the Council in regard to the

appointment of officers. Travers Hartley was elected president at a meeting of the Council on 22 March, and Daniel Marston one of the vice-presidents, but the remaining two offices were reserved for Catholic and Quaker merchants: Joshua Pim was chosen as treasurer and Anthony McDermott, the most senior of the Catholic members, as the other vice-president. Anthony McDermott died within the year, and another Catholic, Denis Thomas O'Brien, was selected to succeed him as vice-president.

The Council was extremely active in its first year, meeting virtually every week, sometimes even more often. The large size of the Council meant in practice that it could never achieve a full turnout of members, but it could on occasion have as many as 25 as at the important meeting on 10 October 1783. The first external issue to face it — its immediate concern had been to sort out the finances of the building of the Exchange — was the Portugal trade. Although the prohibition on the export of woollens from Ireland had been removed in 1779, to the dismay of Irish merchants and politicians alike the Portuguese court was not prepared to alter its commercial arrangements with the British king to accept Irish woollens as being comprehended within the trade. In April the Council had before it a letter from a merchant in Oporto setting out the problems in the trade, and it resolved to present an

(top, from left): George II farthing, 1760; George III halfpenny, 1769; (below): George III penny, 1805.

address to the Lord Lieutenant on the subject. The address was presented by the president and the two vice-presidents, the fact itself stressing that the Council's Catholic vice-president was fully part of its public image. In September it again resolved to address the Lord Lieutenant 'relative to the difficulties still existing with respect to the admission of several of the manufactures of Ireland into Portugal'. The Council also maintained a correspondence with merchants in other Irish ports, and its ambitions for reform were high. Excessive custom house fees, that bugbear of eighteenth- and nineteenth-century merchants, came up at an early date, and Joshua Pim, through the good offices of a Cork co-religionist, George Newsom, was able to put before the Council 'three books containing the proceedings of the Merchants of Cork' in relation to the same matter. Confident of its prospects, the Council did not hesitate to recommend to the well established and highly successful Cork committee that 'institutions similar to the Chamber of Commerce of Dublin are earnestly recommended to the other ports of this kingdom'. In July the Council received a report from a subcommittee on brokerage, and ordered the practices and recommended charges to be printed and sent to every broker in the port. It proceeded also to appoint a committee to review the rates of brokerage in freighting vessels. It was in communication with the Lord Lieutenant on a number of occasions both in relation to expediting the repeal of war-time controls on the shipment of salted provisions and the administrative control on grain shipments in the near-famine of 1783.

The high optimism that prevailed at the outset was, however, increasingly clouded by evidence of a growing commercial crisis. In the spring hopes existed for a large market for Irish goods across the Atlantic in America, and for early access to the Portuguese market. Indeed on 29 April members of the Council were requested to write to their correspondents in various countries for an account of what 'manufactures of the loom' were imported, and also for details of charges, prices, breadth, length and make-up of cloth along with samples. By May the Council had samples of the cloth most in demand in Portugal and the Quaker house of Joseph and Samuel Grubb in Clonmel had sent up samples of what they could provide. But the expected developments did not materialise. By June, glut had set in on the American market, and the Portuguese obstinately refused to open their ports to Irish manufactures. The worsening situation had already been anticipated in a concern with monetary matters in the spring. A report from a sub-committee on the 'present circulating coin of the kingdom' was submitted in April, and more ominously on 31 May the Council declared that 'the payment of inland bills of exchange and promissory notes in the city of Dublin is conducted with great want of punctuality . . .' Evidence of an acute credit crisis can be seen, for instance, in the letter book of John Blake, a prominent Dublin merchant with interests in beef and wool as well as the wine trade. Credit became progressively tighter as the year went by. In September and early October the committee met on average twice a week, dispensing with its formal procedures in order to debate the matter more fully as a committee of the house. Finally, at a very well-attended meeting on 10 October, when those present included Edward Byrne, the sugar refiner, and Robert Brooke, the great cotton manufacturer at Prosperous, both of whom were rarely seen at meetings, a resolution was passed:

> That the languid state of several of the manufactures of this kingdom and the distress of its manufacturers evince that protection is necessary and therefore in the opinion of this committee an addition should be made to the duties at present payable on the importation of several species of manufactures.

A feeling of gloom had now replaced the optimism of the early months. It was determined at the end of October to present a petition to parliament: 'Moved by the distress of multitudes of their fellow citizens . . .', the Chamber requested parliament to review 'the present depressed state of various of the manufactures of this city and kingdom'. The depression was made all the more serious by the poor harvest of 1782 which led to near-famine conditions in the spring of 1783, followed by another bad harvest in the same year. In November and December the Council looked at the grain trade. Like other observers it felt that the import duties remained too high to admit imports readily as grain prices on the Irish market soared, and its petition, like other representations made to the parliament, referred to 'the famine that very lately threatened this kingdom (and averted only by the strong though expedient measures of government) to prove the necessity of reducing the standard of prices at which the present act admits the importation of foreign corn and flour at low prices . . .'

Depression lasted well into 1784, and at popular level agreements took shape against imports of manufactures. Even before the political and social tensions of 1784 had emerged fully, however, bad business conditions had taken a toll of the optimism of Council members. A minute on 20 December 1783, calling a special meeting 'to take into consideration the expediency of enforcing a more punctual and regular attendance of its members', tells its own tale. Some divisions had also emerged among the Chamber's members which further worsened its plight. The powerful wine trade was never well represented among the members of the Council. Wine merchants not only importing wine wholesale but also retailing it in large quantities to peers and rich gentry were much less radical than other merchants, and shared the fear of the more conservative members of the landed classes that revolution could go too far, a fear which was much more evident in 1783 than in the heady days of 1782. The Council represented wholesale merchants, and it was anxious that it should not be infiltrated by less prestigious trades. At a meeting on 13 January 1784 a resolution from a committee on membership included the proposal that 'every person who sells or disposes of any goods or merchandise save and except wines in any other than the package said goods or merchandise is imported in ought to be deemed and considered a retailer'. However, at the meeting the clause 'save and except wines' was deleted. The original proposal from the committee avoided discrimination against the specialist wine merchants who did a retail trade as well as import wines. The resolution as amended in the course of the meeting was itself rejected. However, rejection was due not to the discrimination introduced into the resolution but to the impracticality of one of the other proposals contained in it. The episode hints at a deep and divisive rivalry among merchants themselves. The second year's elections in 1784 to the Council show how far support for the Chamber had receded. Whereas the highest ballot in 1783 had been 153, it was only 36 on this occasion, and in 1784 only 109 members paid their subscription. Thirty-two of the members elected in 1783 were re-elected, and the poll was headed by a Catholic and a Quaker; Denis Thomas O'Brien and Joshua Pim, each with 36 ballots. Moreover, although the total number of voters can not have been very large, the distribution of votes was much more bunched than in the previous year, in which they had been distributed across a wide spectrum. No less than 26 of the 41 members were elected with between 36 and 30 ballots each , suggesting that a large proportion of members present submitted virtually identical ballot papers. In fact the membership of the Council cannot have greatly fallen short of the attendance at the electoral assembly. In 1784 some very significant members either dropped out or failed to get re-elected: George Godfrey Hoffmann, Jeremiah Vickers, Alderman George Sutton, William Alexander, John Allen, Patrick Bride and Robert Brooke. These were all prominent figures, most of whom had polled well in 1783. Moreover, no less than four of them were associated with or to become associated with the Bank of Ireland as directors. The same officers were elected as in 1783 with Denis Thomas O'Brien replacing the deceased McDermott.

The 1784 elections seem to have been the last, as no details of later elections were recorded in the minutes. Support was now smaller than the number of seats on the Council, and the Chamber consisted for all practical purposes of those members who chose to support it. In this disappointing situation formal appointment to offices ceased as well, and the officers seem to have remained those members appointed in 1784. The Committee had become a more radical body than in the past. On several occasions in 1784 it expressed the view that Ireland should be put on a no less advantageous footing than Britain as far as trade was concerned, and in 1785 its proceedings were dominated by consideration of the celebrated Commercial Propositions which were proposed by the British prime minister, William Pitt, as a means of putting trade between the two kingdoms on an equitable basis. The excitement was immense in the early meetings in February: one meeting was recorded as ending at two in the morning. The radical turn of the Chamber is reflected in its meeting with a deputation from the textile manufacturers on 10 February. Manufacturers were distinctly more radical than merchants and were closely identified with the demand for protective duties. The deputation was headed by the Catholic worsted manufacturer Richard McCormick and by two others, William Arnold and James Williams. Indeed, one of the officers of the Chamber, Denis Thomas O'Brien, was himself in the process of moving into cotton manufacture in a big way at Balbriggan. McCormick referred to a prohibition in the Propositions on the export of wool to Ireland. He was otherwise happy. Arnold disagreed. The Council observed that resolutions providing for equal duties on both sides did not in themselves provide an equal measure of protection. Ireland's manufactures were to a great degree in coarser goods than England's and hence the weight of import duties would penalise them more. The Council decided that it was opposed to any export restrictions on trade from one country to the other, and that if they were continued, it would be impolitic for Ireland to forego the right to introduced similar prohibitory measures. The Propositions as sent back in June from the British parliament to the Irish parliament had been made still less attractive. The Council drew up an address on 9 June to circulate to merchants in other ports asking them to petition parliament to ensure that the voice of merchants received as much attention in the Irish parliament as that of British merchants opposed to the measures had in the British. Over the next three months the Council met not less than 35 times. A petition for signature by traders drawn up and approved on 6 August was political in tone, regarding the measures as 'manifestly unjust in their commercial operation and in their political object highly insulting to the dignity of this free nation in as much as they must be subversive of the independency of its legislature'.

However, it did not prove necessary for the Chamber to proceed with the petition, as in August the Irish parliament itself rejected the measure. On 22 August the Chamber approved an address of thanks not to the parliament but to what it described as 'the members of the minority of the House of Commons'. In other words the Chamber identified itself totally with the minority among the 300 members who had espoused the cause of radical and independent reform. The Chamber's address was intended to:

> return their sincere and grateful acknowledgements to the 110 faithful and independent representatives of the people through whose virtue and firmness a measure has been withdrawn which upon mature consideration appears to this Council to have been pregnant with the most injurious consequences . . .

The Council, which could still frequently command as many as twenty members for a meeting, was, by identifying itself so openly with the opposition in Commons, creating friction among its dwindling supporters. It may be suspected that Travers Hartley, who was a member of parliament, was primarily responsible for this development. These politics came into the open in January 1786, triggered by the final stages in the passage through parliament of a bill setting up the Corporation for Preserving and Improving the Port of Dublin, or Ballast Office. The intention of the bill was to put the administration of the port of Dublin on a more effective basis and to create a new and less unrepresentative body to administer its affairs. On 28 January, at a poorly attended meeting with only twelve members present, it was decided to summon a meeting for the following Tuesday to consider providing money to defray costs in supporting the passage of the bill. At this later meeting 22 members were present. Proceedings started with a resolution to expunge the preceding meeting's resolution from the record as reflecting 'upon the public spirit and good sense of the Council'. This resolution declared the bill to be 'patronised by certain men who the Council have reason to think have never been distinguished as the assertors of either the constitutional rights or commercial interests of the kingdom, a bill whose progress through the house was opposed in every stage as unjust in its principles by our worthy president whose judgement, public spirit and impartiality as senator is held in the highest estimation by every honest Irishman'. In comparing the attendance at both meetings some clue is forthcoming as to the source of the division. The attendance at the meeting on 28 January was itself liberal in outlook, although, as it included Pim in the chair, and the attendance numbered merchants as important in the city's life as Crosthwait, Forbes, Marston, and Isaac Weld, the decision was a sober and responsible one. Not all the members present on 31 January who had been absent from the preceding meeting were radicals; it must be suspected that the tone of violent opposition may have been interjected by William Cope or James Hartley, possibly though less likely by Robert Black, Samuel Dick or Thomas Mitchell. That the radicals were not the only ones spoiling for a fight, however, is evident from the progress of the meeting. Although the radical resolution was rejected, when a resolution was put forward naming stated members of the Council as trustees for the £150 to be applied to the cause of the bill, an amendment was proposed adding Lord Ranelagh, John Beresford, John Foster and John Monck Mason to the trustees. These were not only prominent members of the administration, but the obnoxious four nominations to the new harbour Corporation contained in the bill, none of them, it need hardly be said, members of the Chamber. This amendment was rejected, but the violence of the meeting is illustrated both by the furious start to the proceedings and by the final amendment proposed which was in effect a declaration of political defiance against the liberal group. It is not possible to determine with certainty who proposed this amendment, but it is plausible to conjecture that it may have been D'Olier, who had not been present on 28 January and who ceased to attend meetings henceforward.

The Chamber was now in crisis, a fact reflected in a resolution passed at a meeting on 10 December 1787 with 12 members present that 'the continuation and support of a mercantile association in this city is essential to the interests of the merchants of Dublin and of importance to the trade of Ireland'. In the following week the Council was at work as a committee on a report 'relative to the continuation and support of a mercantile association in this city'. Proposals from the committee came before the Council on 22 December: the Chamber was henceforth to be styled 'The Chamber of Commerce of the city of Dublin', and the subscription was to be two guineas. It was decided that members not paying their subscription by 1 February would be deemed to have withdrawn. But the response was poor. In desperation on 30 January it was resolved as 'an instruction to the Secretary that he send around to the members for their subscriptions'. Even though the deadline was extended, no general meeting was called. There were nine meetings of the Council between January and March, and they could only muster from five to twelve members. In these discouraging circumstances the meeting of 29 March 1788 was not

followed by another until 25 February 1791, which proved to be the last recorded in the minutes. It may however, have been followed by another as the proceedings of the meeting of 25 February were signed: J. Patrick; but there must have been no further meeting as the proceedings of that at which Patrick appended his signature are not recorded in the minute book. The Chamber seems to have expired simply through lack of support.

In 1788 the Chamber was reduced to a handful of members: Pim, Crosthwait, the two Hartleys, the two Maquays, Forbes, Gough, Henrick, Williams, Geale, Ramadge, Rawlins, Colvill, Marston, Lindsay, Crothers, Dick, Mitchell, Jaffray junior, Black, Cope and Binns. No Catholic was recorded after O'Brien and O'Connor ceased to appear after 9 January 1788 until Byrne's partner Randal McDonnell was present on 25 February 1791.

The proceedings had now become quite marginal. At least one decision was quite eccentric for a group of merchants who should have favoured lower interest rates. On 14 February 1788 the Council opposed the reduction in the legal rate of interest which the Administration proposed. Borrowers among the gentry and peerage were against this because they feared that if the rate was reduced to the same level as in England they might have difficulty in raising money on mortgages of their land. It is possible to see in this the influence of the Duke of Leinster and the radical political interest around him. Opposition represented at one and the same time landed self-interest and the rejection of Foster's economic policy. Travers Hartley himself was a poor attender at these meetings. He presided on 9 January, but did not appear again until a meeting on 26 March 'summoned to meet to take into consideration the slave trade'. He was in the chair three days later when a resolution was passed that

> The Chamber of Commerce of the city of Dublin having observed with much satisfaction the generous disposition prevalent among their fellow subjects in Great Britain to effect an abolition of the slave trade, a disposition so congenial to the character of a human and enlightened nation and at the same time having indulged themselves in the reflection that the traffic in the human species does not appear to have been ever carried on from this kingdom, yet wishing to be in any degree assistant to the great and good work so relieving numbers of their fellow creatures and desirous that any apprehension of this country engaging in that odious traffic may be obviated have deemed it expedient to come to the following resolutions . . .

There were eight members at this meeting; apart from Hartley, the Quaker Pim and near-Quaker Wilkinson, Crosthwait, Rawlins, Jaffray junior, Cope and Binns.

With the collapse of the Chamber the radical Protestant merchant tradition was almost at an end. Significantly few merchants were among members of the United Irishmen organisation which began in Dublin in 1791, and these few were drawn from a lower level than that of the rich and immensely powerful merchant group who provided the last rump of the Chamber of Commerce. In the course of the 1790s, as fears of revolution spread, merchants became distinctly more conservative. This trend was evident not only among Protestant businessmen but also among Catholics. Malachy O'Connor was the only prominent Catholic merchant to become a member of the United Irishmen, but over the decade the O'Connors, like other businessmen, moved to the right. Edward Byrne, the richest Catholic merchant, while taking a very radical stance on Catholic relief never crossed the border into sedition, and indeed in the Chamber of Commerce was a poor attender, totally unassociated with the increasingly radical views of the Council in the 1780s. His partner, Randal McDonnell, did appear at a meeting in 1791, but 14 years later he seems to have been sufficiently respected by the conservative Protestant businessmen who revived the Chamber to have presided at the first meetings. In the 1790, radicalism took refuge at the level of businessmen among the textile manufacturers of the Liberties, increasingly assailed by competition from English cloth and ready recruits to a social and political stance bitterly opposed to the government and the dominant Foster-Beresford-Fitzgibbon axis in parliament.

When the Chamber was re-established in 1805, it was an entirely new institution with no links with the old one. It got off to a bad start: many of those allowed to ballot at the first meeting in May had not signed the articles

George Adamson,
Ald. William Alexander,
William Alexander,
John Allen,
James Anderson,
Joseph Anderson,
Garret Andrews,
Alexander Armstrong,
Archibald Armstrong,
James Armstrong,
William Arnold,

Joseph Barcroft, jun.
Patrick Bean,
Edward Beatty,
John Binns,
Robert Black,
Hans Blackwood,
Price Blackwood,
Mark Bloxham,
Richard Bolton,
Oliver Bond,
Thomas Bond,
Charles Bourns,
Patrick Bride,
Robert Brooke,
Thomas Digby Brooke,
Richard Brown,
Arthur Bryan,
Patrick Burke,
Thomas Burnett,
Edward Burroughs,
Edmond Byrne,
Edward Byrne,
Joseph Byrne,

Francis Cahill,
Nathaniel Cairns,
William E. Caldbeck,
George Campbell,
James Campbell,
Mathew Cardiff,
John Carleton,
Joseph Church,
Benjamin Clarke,
Charles Clarke,
Hugh Cochran,
John Collins,
Samuel Collins,
William Colvill,
John Comerford,
Valentine Connor,
William Cope,
Michael Cotgrave,
John Costley,
John Cowan,
John Creathorn,
James Crosby,
Leland Crosthwait,
Hugh Crothers,

West Darby,
Ald. John Darragh,
Patrick Deafe,
John Dechuzeau,
Robert Deey,
Jeremiah D'Olier,
David Dick,
Samuel Dick,
Daniel Dickinson,
Joseph Dickinson,
William Dickinson,
Richard Dillon,
William Bruce Dunn,

Richard Eaton,
John English,
George Eskelson,
Patrick Ewing,

Joseph Fletcher,
John Folie,
Edward Forbes,
Joshua Forbes,
William Ford,
Robert Foster,
George Fox,

John Galloway,
Samuel Gamble,
Samuel Garner,
Benjamin Gault,
Daniel Geale,
Ebenezer Geale,
Frederick Geale,
Joseph Geff,
Joshua Green,
Ald. Thomas Green,
Andrew Grehan,
Arthur Guiness,

Hugh Hamill, jun.
Hugh Hamilton,
Robert Hanna,
James Hartley,
Travers Hartley,
John Hetsrick,
George Godfrey Hoffman,
Joseph Hone, jun.
Nathaniel Hone,
Nathaniel Hone, jun.
Ald. James Horan,
Martin Howard,
Peter Howard,
John Hughes,
John Hunt,
Ephraim Hutchinson,

Alexander Jaffray,
Christopher James,
David Jebb.

Caleb Jenkin,
Thomas Jordan, jun.

Patrick Kavenagh,
John Frederick Kelly,
Alex. Kirkpatrick, jun.
Thomas Kirwan,

Henry Lanauze,
George Lamprey,
George Lang,
James Leckey,
Thomas Lee,
John Lindsey,
William Lindsay,
Richard Litton,
Robert Lloyd,
John Locker,
George Lunell,
Ald. Joseph Lynam,
Henry Lyons,

Robert Magee,
Foliott Magrath,
Simon Maguire,
Alexander Maitland,
George Maquay,
Joan Leland Maquay,
James Marsh,
Daniel Mariton,
Andrew Maziere, jun.
Francis M'Annally,
Anthony M'Dermott,
Anthony M'Dermott, jun.
Francis M'Dermott,
Owen M'Dermott,
Patrick M'Laughlin,
Edward Medlicott,
David Melville,
Robert Mercer,
Stephen Miller,
Richard Mitchell,
Thomas Mitchell,
Edward Moore,
Edward Morgan,
Ralph Mulhern,
Denis Murphy,
George Murray,

John Nairne,
William Netterville,
Richard Neville,
John Nevin,
Brabazon Noble,
Richard Nunn,

Charles O'Brien,
Dennis Thomas O'Brien,
Oliver O'Hara,
John Orr.

John James Pache,
George Palmer,
Alexander Patrick,
John Patrick,
Paul Patrick,
William Penrose,
John Phelps,
Joseph Pike.
Joshua Pim,
Michael Plunkett,
Richard Plunkett,
James Potts,
Philip Proffor,

Thomas Rainey,
Smith Ramage,
William Rawlins,
Edward Reynolds,

Robert Shaw,
Ald. James Sheil,
Abraham Skeys,
William Smith,
Robert Smith,
Robert Smith, jun.
William Speer,
Arthur Stanley,
William Stephens,
Robert Stephenson,
James Stewart,
Alexander Stillas,
Amos Strettle,
Ald. George Sutton,
John Sutton, Beresford-street,
Patrick Sweetman,

James Napper Tandy,
William Trocke,
Thomas Tweedy,

Godfrey Vaughan.
Jeremiah Vickers,
Jeremiah Vickers, jun.

Charles Ward,
Rt. Hon. Nathaniel Warren, Lord Mayor,
Isaac Weld,
Luke White,
Robert White,
Abraham Wilkinson,
Peter Wilkinson,
Henry Williams,
James Williams,
Benjamin Wills.
William Wilson,
William Worthington,

Printed by W. WILSON, No. 6, Dame-street.

ROYAL EXCHANGE.

DUBLIN, 7th FEBRUARY, 1783.

At a MEETING of the MERCHANTS of this CITY.

TRAVERS HARTLEY, Esq; in the CHAIR.

A PAPER having been introduced, containing propositions for the establishment of a CHAMBER OF COMMERCE in this City.

RESOLVED,
That the said Paper be referred to the Committee of Merchants, and their opinion thereon be requested.

The Meeting adjourned to Tuesday Evening next, at Seven o'Clock.

FEBRUARY 10th, 1783.

At a MEETING of the COMMITTEE of MERCHANTS, regularly convened by Summons, for the special Purpose of taking into Consideration a Plan for instituting a CHAMBER OF COMMERCE in this City.

WILLIAM COLVILL, Esq; in the CHAIR.

MR. JOHN PATRICK and MR. JOSHUA PIM presented to the Committee the plan hereunto annexed, which being received, read, and considered, the following RESOLUTIONS were entered into.

THAT we highly approve of said plan, as forming a broad and firm foundation on which may be expected to arise a superstructure of eminent usefulness in the commercial department.

THAT from this measure the trading interest is likely to derive great additional importance and respect, and the public in general the advantages consequent thereto.

THAT

First list of subscribers to the Dublin Chamber of Commerce, February 7, 1783.

of association, and a second meeting was held three weeks later. There were 89 present at the first meeting. It is noticeable that the old radical group among the merchants was absent as were in the main the Quakers.

In July 1805 a very cold letter from Joshua Pim was received relating to property of the old Chamber which he held and which he would make over 'as public property . . . and on that condition they are at the service of the' new Chamber. Leland Crosthwait senior, along with Pim one of the mainstays of the Chamber in the 1780s, had no part in the formation of the new Chamber either since he was admitted a member only as late as 25 February 1806. Catholic merchants, on the other hand, were well represented at the meeting. They included Randal McDonnell, the old partner of Edward Byrne, John J. Power from Wexford whose son was to marry into the Talbot family and representing the successful Wexford Catholic business interest in the capital, as well as several O'Connors whose family was to remain identified with conservative Dublin business for several generations. Given the divisions evident in the Dublin merchant community, it is at first sight surprising that a Chamber was founded at all at this stage. The incentive for its establishment seems to have been the question of custom house fees, one of the long standing complaints of merchants, and one of the few issues on which a deeply divided merchant community might find common ground.

Randal McDonnell headed the ballot at both meetings. However, Arthur Guinness, who was only sixth on the first ballot, was second on the later one. This was, in fact very much a conservative Protestant venture. Arthur Guinness the second (son of the Arthur who in a fleeting association had been one of the 293 members in 1783) presided at several of the early meetings of the Council. Richard Darling was elected Treasurer, and Joseph Wilson was elected chairman. It was only when Wilson resigned that the chair was offered to McDonnell who declined, Alderman Hone becoming chairman on 12 July. The insecure position of the new Chamber was reflected in the fact that at the end of December it again requested McDonnell to accept the chairmanship for three months, an offer which he accepted only on 25 February. There is much evidence of difficulty in filling the chair: this was evident in 1805 and was to the fore again in 1806. Although McDonnell was asked to serve for three months, he seems, in fact, to have served for six. In June 1806 Maziere was asked to act as chairman, but there was a succession of persons who took the chair at meetings in July. In January 1807 George Carleton was elected chairman and he presided at meetings as late as January 1809. The undemocratic nature of the Council is reflected also in the fact that 16 of the 21 members were to be elected by the Council itself and only five by the general assembly. The lack of support was such that the Council electoral meeting on 20 May 1806 could not proceed to elections 'the members present being rather too limited for so material a proceeding as the intended election'. At the general meeting on 5 July there were only 29 ballots, and no Quaker presence at all, the solitary Quaker on the preceding year's Council having now disappeared. It was clearly a body with a range of support too narrow to make elections meaningful. The minutes show no evidence of further elections. The fact that the Chamber's support was so narrow suggests why some of its proceedings took the form of meetings of the Council with groups of merchants. In March 1806 six merchants in the West Indian trade attended a

Council meeting and in October 1806 the Council met the butter exporters in a meeting presided over by John Patrick who had been identified with the old Chamber but was not a member of the Council of the new one. In January 1809 the Chamber summoned a general meeting of importers and exporters. This meeting was presided over by Randal McDonnell, and it elected a committee of its own whose membership overlapped with that of the Council. The minute book was extremely badly kept. After the meeting with traders on 14 January, the book records the first part of a meeting of the Council two days later, and then, because a section of the volume is missing, jumps to the recording of the latter part of a ballot held on a date which cannot be specified. A meeting can be identified as having been held on 22 December 1812. It seems to represent some stage in a short-lived rejuvenation of the Council because one of the members of the Council was a Quaker, Thomas Pim, and the meeting dealt with admissions which significantly included two other Quakers, Samuel Bewley and Jonathan Pim. Minutes followed of another meeting a week later, but the absence of further minutes indicates that this timid venture, more broad-based than the narrow Chamber of the intervening years, also quickly came to nought.

V

Revival and expansion
*1820*1875*

The collapse of the Dublin Chamber of Commerce was a striking phenomenon, emphasising how divided the Dublin business community was by what were ultimately religious and political factors. In Cork, by contrast, the Committee of Merchants had continued uninterrupted from 1769, and Belfast's Chamber of Commerce, established also in 1783, though inactive at times, had never suspended its existence. It is clear too that committees existed in Limerick and Waterford by 1805 because in that year the freshly constituted Dublin Chamber consulted them as well as the Cork and Belfast bodies. The absence of a Dublin body could hardly last indefinitely in circumstances where merchants in major ports everywhere were organised for common purposes. What was required was an incentive, and that came characteristically in 1820 over indignation with custom house fees said to amount to an illegal imposition of several thousand pounds per annum. A meeting of merchants took place at the Commercial Buildings on 24 August 1820 to draw up a plan for a Chamber of Commerce. The immediate impulse behind this proposal was a liberal one with links reaching back to the old Chamber of Commerce which had expired in 1791. Randal McDonnell chaired the first two public meetings to institute the Chamber, and the committee of eight formed at the second meeting on 12 October included at least one Catholic from the paper manufacturing McDonnell family and the Quaker J. R. Pim. (This McDonnell family does not appear at first sight to be related to Randal McDonnell.) When a further six members were added to the committee in the course of its work, they included John Lindsay, who had been a member of the old committee in the 1780s, the Quaker Samuel Bewley, and Thomas Crosthwait, indicating that that family was behind the project also. Indeed, at a meeting at the Royal Exchange on 16 November to approve the regulations no less as person than Leland Crosthwait took the chair. The regulations which were approved were more elaborate than those of the past. The annual general assembly should elect a president, four vice-presidents, and committee of 21 members. In a clear effort to prevent the emergence of a self-perpetuating clique, not more than 14 of the 21 members of the preceding council were to be eligible for re-election each year. There should be four general meetings of the Chamber every year, and the Council should meet regularly once a month.

The liberal backing behind the project is reflected in the fact that Joshua Pim was elected first president of the Chamber. He had stood aside from the 1805 project totally, and his election was an indication that the spirit of 1791

rather than that of 1805 ruled. Of the four vice-presidents, two were Randal McDonnell and Leland Crosthwait, and the other two were John Lindsay, who also had associations with the old chamber of 1791, and James Chambers who, while having no clear associations either with the liberal or conservative elements of Dublin business life, may have had, many years before, a United Irishman son. Thirty-seven candidates received ballots for the 21 seats on the Council. Both Bewley and J. R. Pim were among the members elected. Arthur Guinness, who was prominent in 1805, was third last of the 37, receiving a mere 31 votes. In the elections of December 1821 the same balance of forces broadly held, although the threat of incipient politicisation was reflected in the fact that seven candidates emerged for the four posts of vice-president, and Guinness, who polled fourth, became a vice-president (with 31 votes as against 66 for Crosthwait and Lindsay). The attendance was low at the ballot — only 69 were present — and this hardly augured well for the liberals, as unless uncommitted businessmen continued to support the Chamber, it was vulnerable to concerted action by the conservative interest. In March 1823 of the following year (elections having in the interval been transferred from December to March), with a large attendance of 181, Leland Crosthwait was elected president. But two votes were cast for Guinness as president, and the shape of things to come was anticipated in the fact that Guinness headed the poll for vice-president with 160 votes. Broadly the same pattern was reproduced at the meetings in 1824 and 1825. Even as far back as the general meeting of December 1821 the fear of politicisation had been reflected in a resolution that 'a committee of 9 be appointed to consider and devise such eligible measures as by celebrating the formation of this association would be conducive to a continuance of unanimity and good will among the members'. The composition of this committee suggests that this was an initiative by the Quakers, some Catholics and uncommitted established church members. The pattern in the 1821 elections, repeated in March 1823, suggests that the disruption was feared from the direction of Arthur Guinness.

One of the arresting aspects of the Chamber in the 1820s is that its membership held up and grew. One reason for this was the interest taken by businessmen in administrative reform in the 1820s; the other was the issue of politicisation which some members supported, others opposed. The Chamber counted 263 members at the end of 1821 and this number had risen to 462 by December 1825. Little short of 200 members attended the ballot at the end of the annual meetings. Impatience with defective regulations, illegal fees at the custom house and patronage in regulatory office reached a high level. There was nothing novel in this in itself, but businessmen everywhere were now impregnated with the tenets of the new political economy. Significantly in April 1824 the library committee recommended the purchase of Ricardo's *Principles of political economy* and Mill's *Elements of political economy* as well as the more utilitarian works of reference which were the normal staple of business libraries. The Council itself in March 1824 set out its views on regulation of the coal trade:

> All legislative interference to regulate the prices of commodities of general consumption not only fail but act contrary to their purposes. The enlightened views of the present age have discovered that the true mode of encouraging trade and commerce is to free them from those restrictions which a mistaken policy shackled them with heretofore and the application of the doctrine applies in a peculiar degree in the opinion of your committee to the subject under consideration.

The butter trade was a still more important instance of the abuses which merchants faced, and a particularly apposite one because Quakers were deeply involved. The question first came up in an address to the Council in May 1821 from the Quaker town of Mountmellick, which declared that they were obliged to ship their butter through Waterford rather than Dublin, and asked for steps to be taken to put Dublin on the same footing as Cork and Waterford in the branding and inspection of butter. By the end of the year conferences and deputations on the subject had come to nothing, and the general meeting in December was told that 'it speedily appeared that the intangibility of patronage and a tenacious adherence to private interests raised insurmountable obstacles'. So exasperated was opinion on this issue that the officers clearly feared that expectations were too high, and they warned members in 1821 that:

> In thus referring to the legitimate cases, to the advantages that may be *reasonably* expected from associations of this nature, your Council would at the same time endeavour to obviate the effects to which exaggerated conceptions in these respects may have given birth — those amongst us who imagined that the institution was to act as a specific for our commercial complaints, that its establishment would be followed by a radical reform throughout our local departments, reducing all grievances and banishing all abuses, that its influence with miraculous efficacy was to revive the languid and raise the prostrate interests of commerce and counteracting the force of adverse circumstances, to recall the prosperity of former times, assuredly indulged anticipation somewhat inconsistent with the characteristic soberness of his calling, he employed his fancy in erecting a standard the application of which to their unpretending labours your Council would most earnestly deprecate.

By 1823 the Council was in touch with the merchants of other ports and the pressures the Chamber engendered were thus instrumental in the setting up of the parliamentary investigation whose massive report appeared in 1826. The episode is a good instance of the way in which an issue worked its way through society and how reform was brought about. In 1824 the committee was also involved in calling for the repeal of acts affecting the silk trade in Dublin. In the 1820s the Chamber was, of course, swimming with the tide and at the Board of Trade both officials and its political head were in favour of reform, so that the Chamber and other trade bodies could count on a sympathetic hearing to grievances and the prospect of action. Much of the Chamber's work was detailed attention to legislative changes and amendments rather than to broad issues. Some of it involved lobbying in London, and seeking legal advice, and this aspect was to remain throughout the nineteenth century a task which devolved on a handful of members on the Council rather than on the Chamber at large. In a reforming age politicians were prepared to listen to merchants in a way which would have been inconceivable in the past when merchants could only hope to have a condescending audience mingled with social contempt.

Politicisation was the other factor giving the affairs of the Chamber an interest in the 1820s. By 1825 it was very evident, despite the wishes of the Quaker members in particular for a non-politicised body, that the influence of Arthur Guinness was in the ascendant. The rise in membership, moreover, was being drawn from conservative circles. There was a very sustained admission of new members in 1823, and for what appears to have been the first time in the history of the Chamber families like the Bartons and Sneyds were now members. In 1823 Joseph Pim polled very well, though unsuccessfully for office; in 1824 he received a mere 22 votes. It was now clear also that as a result of the rapid rise in membership the general body was more conservative than the Council which was still dominated by prestigious figures from the past like Crosthwait. At the annual meeting in March 1826, though Leland Crosthwait was re-elected, the Guinness faction felt bold enough to raise the question of the need to seek a satisfactory political representation of the business interests, and had a majority for a proposal to hold a special meeting to consider the question. At this meeting William Lunell Guinness was in the chair. The Council reported to the meeting against the idea of political involvement, as it held back the spirit of unanimity. The Council reported that

> It must be recollected also, that the instrumentality of this body, in promoting the object in contemplation must chiefly be exercised, through the moral influence which may be produced by a public declaration in favour of some individual; but from the causes to which we have adverted it can scarcely be hoped that any such declaration would go forth with that stamp of unanimity, or be sustained by that general and cordial concurrence even amongst ourselves . . .

The Council mentioned how from the start it had maintained strict neutrality: 'in no single instance have they violated this principle'. It went on to deprecate any means calculated to interrupt 'the harmony hitherto subsisting amongst us', and deviation from the principle would 'not only be the certain prelude of our separation, but must render their separation an event in every respect desirable'. A proposal against political involvement was put forward by Vance and seconded by J. R. Pim. It was carried and published in the newspapers. Though defeated for the moment, the opportunity for Guinness to put himelf forward came quicker than anticipated. Crosthwait died in the middle of the year, and a special meeting was called for 20 June. At this the 41 members present unanimously elected Guinness president. It seems likely that the hint in the Council report had been translated into action, and that the liberal members stayed away as a form of abstensionism. That this is the case is borne out by the election in March 1827 when at a meeting at which 167 were present, Guinness received 167 ballots, the members of the Council all receiving 162 or more. Such a result could only have been achieved in circumstances in which the meeting was packed with supporters and others abstained. Again in March 1828, when only 56 members voted, all 26 officers and Council members had 55 or 56 votes. It seems likely that, in his bid to take over the Chamber, Guinness had recruited over the years a large number of members to secure his eventual election. Significantly, in the months after his first election as a vice-president, recruitment to the Chamber rose at a very rapid rate: membership growing from 310 in December 1822 to 462 in December 1825. A high level of recruitment in the years after 1826 may have been intended to secure this control, the membership peaking at 619 in 1832 after which it began to fall. The purely political nature of Guinness's interest is reflected in his poor attendance record which contrasted with that of preceding officers. After his first election in 1821 to Council he was an infrequent attender at Council meetings, and although he had become president in June 1826 he first took the chair at a general meeting in March 1828.

A handful of members returned to the Council in and after 1826 were Catholics and Quakers. It seems fairly clear that some form of arrangement implicitly or explicitly must have been patched up with the rampant unionists in 1826. In the case of the few Catholic families on it such as the O'Briens, O'Connors and McDonnells, there may have been no great

problem: propertied Catholics were becoming allies in the large sense, although very guarded ones, of the unionists. Moreover, Guinness himself favoured Catholic Emancipation, and pragmatically in 1831 supported the Reform Bill. In the case of the Quakers a tacit understanding may have been reached between the two sides: acceptance of unionist dominance in return for some place on the Chamber's Council. But it is quite astonishing how unrepresented Catholics and Quakers were among the officers of the Chamber. Often very prominent in the Dublin business world, a fact reflected even in their access to the board of directors of the increasingly unionist Bank of Ireland, they ceased to hold any of the offices of the Chamber of Commerce. After the disappearance of Samuel Bewley who had remained treasurer until 1837, Quakers or Catholics were very rarely chairmen, in the absence of the President, of the poorly attended general meetings of the Chamber. In other words, and quite in contrast with the traditions of the past the Chamber had become a narrow and increasingly exclusive unionist enclave. This lack of influence is particularly striking in the case of the Quakers. Not only had they been the main force in creating the Chamber in 1783 and in reconstituting it in 1820, but in the 1830s and 1840s they were the most vital single force in Dublin business life. Even more than in the past, this was the great period of the Pims. In the eighteenth century they had dominated the worsted trade,

The port of Dublin: South Wall Lighthouse, by W. H. Bartlett, 1842.

63

and by the early nineties, though they did not convert their house into a bank, they handled the Dublin financial business of many country merchants. It was the Pims, with the temporary support of Lancashire capital, who created the Royal Bank in 1836. It was to be considered later as the best-run of the Dublin banks and throughout the nineteenth century it was to remain the bank of Dublin wholesale business. In the same decade as the Pims created the Royal, Jonathan Pim launched the railway age in Ireland with the Dublin & Kingstown which was to be run with a remarkable mercantile flair in the effort to build up traffic. Another Quaker family, the Perrys, were promoters of mainline railways, and shared the Irish railway world with William Dargan, who had become involved in railway construction. Yet none of these men held any position in the Chamber of Commerce. The contrast in social values between Guinness and Dargan is perhaps aptly illustrated in the latter's declining the offer of a baronetcy in 1853 from Queen Victoria when she visited Ireland to open the great Exhibition which he had masterminded.

It may be asked why businessmen remained members of the Chamber during this dismal period in its history. The answer is in large measure that the Chamber still managed to do good work. This was made easier by the constitution adopted in 1820 which produced a relatively small Council in place of the unwieldly one of the past. Month after month its members worked at the humdrum task of considering the mailboat service, postal communication, legislation, fiscal changes, relations with the Ballast Office. The details are set out in the annual reports, the first of which appeared in

Headquarters of the Royal Bank of Ireland, Foster Place, Dublin.

64

1821 and then continued almost without fail, in itself an achievement indicating that a new momentum had been created. While few of the items reported can be described as exciting, the changes which were taking place were the vital ones in Dublin and in the business world around the Irish Sea. Merchants could also now take it for granted that their voice would be listened to by politicians, and the Dublin Chamber was but one of a number in both Ireland and Britain establishing a channel of ideas and representations from the business world to the administrative one. Humdrum though much of this activity might have been, it was an essential part of the dense network of human relationships that made up the changing fabric of the nineteenth century. Essentially the Chamber for its effectiveness depended on the work of a handful of devoted members of the Council, and the voluminous minutes are the record of this labour of love, for such it was for the individual members who gave so much of their time with little prospect of tangible benefit for themselves or their own businesses. A good case in point is Samuel Bewley who remained treasurer until 1837 despite the enormous strain that the changes in 1826-7 must have placed on his loyalty. Another instance of a loyal member is George Drevar. While not a member of the Quaker-liberal group, his personal standing was such that in 1821 he received the largest number of ballots for the Council, becoming a vice-president in 1825 and serving in the same role in the second half of the decade. More crucial still in the day-to-day working of the Chamber was Charles Haliday, who, becoming a member of the Council in 1832, served as secretary from the same year, and became vice-president in 1849. The labours of men such as this ensured that, despite the political strains that the change in the 1820s caused, members of the business community supported the Chamber for the good work it did in practical issues that concerned businessmen. If it had failed to do so, the Quaker threat in 1826 that those opposed to politicisation would leave would probably have been carried out.

Another result was that there was enough of a political opposition in the Chamber to prevent the identification with the unionists from becoming total. This was very evident from events in 1830 when the highly partisan Council passed a resolution thanking the conservative member of parliament for Dublin for his services to the Chamber, but not the liberal representative, for the same constituency, Henry Grattan's son. A special meeting of the Chamber was immediately summoned on a requisition signed by 39 members regarding 'the merits of a resolution entered into by the Council and addressed to George Ogle Moore, and the propriety of including our faithful, tried and incorruptible representative Mr. Grattan in the compliment conferred by that resolution'. The secretary's statement to the meeting, which was intended to explain the situation, if anything simply confirmed the close links between some members of the Council and the unionist representative:

> Soon after Mr. Moore's return to Dublin it was mentioned in the course of casual conversation which occurred with certain members of the Council that they had reason to think that a very general feeling of satisfaction existed among the mercantile classes at his attention to their application on commercial affairs and the general solicitude he had evinced to forward their interests and comply with their wishes . . . The individuals to whom this observation was addressed did not feel

Original second class carriage, Dublin and Kingstown Railway. From **The Dublin Penny Journal,** *1835.*

themselves justified, perhaps they did not think that it would much redound to the credit of this body for respectability or independence to say to Mr. Moore that although they believed that the merchants of Dublin approved of his conduct, yet it was unreasonable to expect that they would give expression to that opinion — or do the only thing that could condone their approbation of any importance. They told him that the subject should be regularly brought before the Council and the results communicated to him — a notice was issued accordingly and a meeting was held at which the following resolution was passed . . .
This resolution was passed without a dissenting voice, every individual present expressing his full concurrence in the proposition itself — and although some diversity of opinion existed and some discussion took place as to the time and mode of presenting it to Mr. Moore yet no substantive resolution was proposed at variance with that which in accordance with the intentions of the majority of the members there present was actually adopted.

The secretary defended the decision further by saying that they had had no request from Mr. Grattan. He attempted to score the point that 'the personal attendance of that gentleman in parliament was less interrupted than that of his colleague and on some occasions when matters of considerable [blank] to our trading interest were pending he was absent', and that if they had taken other things into account they would be open to the accusation 'of converting a commercial society into a political club'. He denied that the resolution was 'intended to serve an electioneering purpose'. The upshot of the discussion was that a resolution was passed thanking both representatives and declaring that both were 'justly entitled to our best support at the approaching election'. It was a defeat for the unionist faction, although given their dominant position it also reflected a preparedness to compromise rather than totally polarise the Chamber: it did not alter the balance of power in any way. Arthur Guinness was unanimously re-elected president every single year from 1826 to 1855; in most years the Council seem to have been elected unanimously as well. Apart from 1831 and 1834 there seem to have been contested elections only in 1841. In that year 55 ballots were apparently cast on a block basis by the unionist members. Fifty-five ballots were cast for the president and four vice-presidents; the same number of votes were cast for 14 Council members and 54 for another three Council members. Thus the five officers and 17 Council members can be identified as the unionist block, and the remaining members can be regarded as the members who were not part of the unionist machine. Significantly, no Quakers were elected to the Council between 1840 and 1844: it is likely that they were absent from the ballot sessions in those years. Quakers re-appeared only in 1845; in 1847 they seem to have forced an election: Thomas Bewley stood unsuccessfully for the office of vice-president.

It is hardly surprising that in such an atmosphere of party domination of the affairs of the Chamber, its administrative standards should tend to fail. No report would seem to have been prepared in 1844. No meeting was held in March in many years. In 1855 the annual general meeting did not take place until May, and indeed in the two preceding years the annual general meeting was also later then its March date. From 1860 onwards the annual general meeting of the Chamber was held in June or July, although this departure from the Chamber's own constitution was formally approved only in July 1867. The perfunctory spirit in which the Chamber at large was treated is amply confirmed in the report of the 1865 annual general meeting held on 4 July when the chairman told the gathering 'that he had been desired by the Council to state to the meeting that no subjects requiring any special report had come under their consideration during the past year, and that he would therefore only request attention to the usual statement of accounts.' Guinness's last appearance in the chair as president at a general meeting was in April 1853 although he continued to be elected president as late as 1855. He was followed by Thomas Crosthwait in 1857. Guinness had in fact died in 1855, but no general meeting or election was held in 1856, and Crosthwait presided over meetings in his capacity as vice-president until the general meeting of March 1857.

The pattern of long presidencies persisted. Crosthwait remained president until 1870 and his successor, William Digges La Touche, was president for 11 years. The Chamber sank to even lower depths in these years. In December 1873, at a special meeting called to deal with a railway bill, the secretary informed the meeting that 'the annual general assembly had not been held owing to a severe accident which had happened to himself and which would have prevented him from attending'. Quite apart from the assumption that it could not take place without the secretary's presence, it illustrates how exclusively the Chamber's functioning was in the hands of its officers. The meeting agreed moreover to the existing Council continuing until the next annual general meeting, a decision which according to the minutes was greeted with acclamation. Earlier in January 1873 the ten members to represent the Chamber on a Corporation Committee about Dublin's gas supply were suggested to the Chamber by the Council: they were a very selective group drawn from Dublin big business and banking, including no less a person than Colvill, at the time governor of the Bank of Ireland. There were no Quakers and, as far as can be judged, no Catholics— or perhaps one.

Sir Benjamin Lee Guinness, Bart. (1798- 1868), third son of the second Arthur and on whom the sole ownership of the brewery devolved c.1858.

Moreover, this narrow composition was decided on despite the fact that the non-establishment members took a keen interest in matters concerning the corporation or the Ballast Office. A special meeting had been summoned in January 1866 regarding the Ballast Office on the requisition of 43 members. Another was summoned in February in dissatisfaction with the Council as much as the Ballast Office. The January requisition related to tolls, a matter which united many members of the Chamber, the resolution being proposed by Benjamin Guinness and seconded by Jonathan Pim. The following meeting was more overtly political, because it sprang from dissatisfaction not only with the Ballast Office opposition to wider representation on its Board, based on the specious ground that, as it controlled the lighthouse department continuity of representation would have to be assured, but with the Council's acceptance of the Ballast Office's case. This meeting was requisitioned by no less than 64 members. They all had non-establishment names, and Quakers and Catholics were prominent among them. For the first time since 1830 there was real confrontation at a meeting. There were two resolutions, one proposed by the chairman adopting the Council's report, another proposed by William Watson and seconded by Richard Kelly, declaring the offer from the Ballast Office to be 'unsatisfactory' and the reasons 'intolerable'. The minutes speak tersely of a stormy meeting: 'after a lengthened discussion, Mr. Watson withdrew the amendment with permission of the meeting'.

In January 1867 a further special meeting was forced on the Council, this time summoned by 38 members including James McDonnell, George Kinahan and William Findlater. Some regular opposition was now beginning to emerge in the Chamber. A change in the hours of opening of the Chamber was opposed at a special meeting in 1868, although the opposition did not press its case after it had been 'fully discussed'. The days of the old hegemony were numbered, although perhaps few, if any on either side can have realised this in 1867-8. Or perhaps they did, as the Ballast Office seemed very much on the defensive, exhorting 'that the Board as well as the public should hesitate to afford justification or pretext for any further attempts at the system of centralisation which has already produced results so detrimental to the interest of Ireland'. Many prominent business people, although like Charles Eason they joined the Chamber, stood aside from its activities altogether. Unionist politicians, including Benjamin Lee Guinness who eventually became a member of parliament, were disliked by such individuals, and it was only with the serious threat of home rule from the 1880s that some degree of general cohesion began to emerge in the ranks of Protestant businessmen.

VI

The eclipse of the merchant
1876*1919

Dublin grew steadily. By 1911 the built-up area had a population of 400,000, over twice the figure of 1800. Its expansion had far exceeded the municipal boundaries of the city, and the shift to the suburbs accelerated over time as transport services — railways, horse-drawn buses, followed by trams — were developed. The main thrust of comfortable living was now concentrated on the adjoining independent townships of Rathmines, Pembroke and Blackrock. The consequence was the emergence of a sharp contrast between the poverty evident at the centre and an impressive amount of new and large housing on the outer fringes of the city. Housing statistics for the city within the municipal limits overstate the poverty of the city, because they do not include the suburbs in which, after 1850, the bulk of new residential construction took place. As municipal boundaries began to lose their original coherence, the contrast lay between a

Trams at Ballsbridge, Dublin, c.1904. The line from Haddington Road to Blackrock, via Ballsbridge, was authorised under a Tramways act of 1878 empowering the Dublin Southern Districts Tramway Co. to construct lines of 5ft. 3in. guage. The Dublin United Tramways Co., formed in 1881, took over 32 miles of line and 137 horse tramcars. The first electric car ran from Ballsbridge to Dalkey on May 16, 1896. The last horse tram in Dublin ran to Sandymount on January 13, 1901. The very last Dublin tram, excluding the Hill of Howth service, ran from Nelson Pillar to Dalkey on July 10, 1949.

high-rated city, inhabited increasingly by the poorer sections of the population and unable to afford the costs of infrastructural development, and low-rated suburbs inhabited by a growing proportion of the city's well-off. Municipal reform was an obvious requirement, but the prospect of reform was complicated by the emerging political divide between the Corporation, which became nationalist, and the townships which were unionist. Taken as a whole the city was much less poor than figures for the municipal area alone suggest. It prospered as a commercial centre and, as the comfortable residential districts to the south testified, many drew substantial incomes from commerce and service industries.

In the nineteenth century Dublin lost the bulk of its textile industries once located in the Liberties or in mills along the streams flowing into the Liffey. It also lost some of the national wholesale role it had held in the eighteenth century as new wholesalers arose in Belfast, Cork and some of the larger inland towns. These wholesalers were facilitated by the great improvement in transport created by the railway network after the 1840s. In the centre, moreover, even if housing was increasingly taken over as tenements for the working classes, commercial development intensified as the middle classes moved out. From the middle of the century Sackville Street (O'Connell Street) was rapidly developing into a commercial district of large shops and business premises, and a similar sustained process took place on the south side in Grafton Street, Dame Street and South Great George's Street. These shops catered for a clientele drawn from the city and suburbs and to some extent from the country as a whole as no other city had a comparable range of wholesale and retail facilities. Even if Dublin wholesalers lost relatively to wholesalers elsewhere, they compensated in part through the rise in sheer volume in the second half of the century. Moreover, in some commodities such as tea, where a mass market grew only after the middle of the century, established wholesalers in Dublin were in a position to serve a national market. No less than two of the Chamber of Commerce presidents were tea merchants (John Bagot, 1882-4 and Edward H. Andrews, 1918), and this does not include two other business families who developed a large tea business, Bewleys and Findlaters. Again, independent wholesalers elsewhere imported much of their goods through Dublin, partly because the transport system was centred on the city, partly because Liverpool was becoming the main centre of much of English overseas trade and Dublin's proximity to Liverpool meant that goods transshipped there for Ireland could conveniently be forwarded through Dublin. The consequence was that even where wholesale trade was transferred from Dublin account to country account, goods for the midlands, west and south continued to be consigned to Dublin and transferred to the railways there. This entailed a vast amount of unskilled labour in cartage, storage and warehousing. The shipping, railway and banking concerns based on Dublin gained not only from enterprise in the capital itself but from the success of businessmen in the small towns and the countryside. Moreover, while Dublin's direct trade ties with other countries declined, transshipment in Liverpool gave a boost to cross-channel shipping: interests in cross-channel shipping became a very important dimension of Dublin business life.

Dublin as a business centre thus had much vitality in the second half of the

century. It was increasingly congested by the growth of commercial traffic: this was reflected in the development of the dock area in which the Chamber of Commerce took a continuing interest. It was also reflected in new central thoroughfares to ease traffic such as Butt Bridge and the adjoining Tara Street which were intended to carry cross-river traffic from the north and south quays to the growing business districts on both sides of the river. On the south side congestion, especially in traffic destined for the business districts off Thomas Street and James's Street, was also evident at the end of Dame Street. Hence the Chamber in 1879 was a strong partisan of 'the formation of a wide and convenient street with an easy gradient from Dame Street to Christ Church Place . . . having regard to the present and every-day increasing trade of the city'. A Dublin businessman of the second half of the nineteenth century would not have thought of his city in terms of the decline and depression in which it is painted in many retrospective accounts. Its drink industries were famous. The St. James's Gate Brewery of Arthur Guinness Son & Company was becoming recognised as the greatest in the world. Its distilleries too produced a famous pot-still whiskey which was more widely marketed across the world than Scotch and the prestige of this product was one of the factors which in the long run prevented Dublin distillers from exploiting the market for cheap patent whiskey on which the

71

growth of Scotch was to be based. Jacob's biscuit factory, established in 1853 by a Waterford Quaker family who moved to Dublin, gradually built up a world-wide renown: by 1917 it employed 3,000 workers. The city's United Tramway Company was the pioneer of electrical traction within the British Isles. Its contracting enterprise had long been famous. William Dargan, elected a member of the Ouzel Galley in 1853, had been contractor to many of the Irish railway companies, and in the closing decades of the century William Martin Murphy, who despite his many business interests, regarded himself first and foremost as a railway contractor, was to build railways and tramways in several parts of the world. Almost symbolically the city hall in Belfast, the civic embodiment of that city's wealth in the 1890s, was erected by the Dublin contracting firm of H. and J. Martin, who also built the main drainage systems of both Dublin and Belfast.

In the middle decades of the century the dominant business interests had not yet changed radically, and they still revolved around the old families who had risen in the world as general merchants in wholesale and foreign trade. This is reflected too in the fact that a Crosthwait: Thomas, son of Leland Crosthwait, was president of the Chamber of Commerce from 1857 to 1870, and that in 1871 the presidency reverted for a decade to the representative of an even older family, William Digges La Touche. In the 1850s and 1860s the Chamber was still dominated by old families. In 1862, for instance, no less than 11 of the 26 members who constituted the officers and Council were drawn from families which had been prominent in the city's trade in the eighteenth century, and most of the remaining members were from families

already prominent for a generation or two in the city's business. Such families had also close ties with the banking world, and no less than seven of the members in 1862 had banking interests or directorships. It was thus a very narrow world of old-established business and wealth.

The wholesalers of the past were not only wholesalers but *merchant* wholesalers. Their function invariably meant that they either engaged in foreign trade or had a provincial custom as well as a local one. Moreover, in the age before widespread banking they often played a banking role as well and if engaged in overseas trade, in many instances had shipping interests of their own and as a community provided their own insurance cover. The essence of the mid-nineteenth century changes was the eclipse of the merchant. As communications improved, both wholesalers and manufacturers could dispense with the services of the merchant as an intermediary. Typically, he had handled both exports and imports, and if he specialised at all, he did so more in a market-area than in a commodity. If merchant houses survived, it was by conversion into a wholesale house in a single commodity. Moreover, both wholesaler and merchant were now frequently overshadowed by manufacturers in wealth and prestige. The Guinnesses progressed to the peerage and to London social life in conservative political circles. No wholesaler rivalled the Jamesons, the distillers, in prestige by the end of the century. As trade and wealth grew,

Pim's department store, Georges Street, Dublin, in the early 1900s. The building has since been demolished.

73

Joseph Todhunter Pim, born July 12, 1841 at Kingstown (Dun Laoghaire), was Deputy-Governor of the Bank of Ireland and chairman of Pim Brothers Ltd.

retailers too emerged from obscurity often to play a prominent role in local business life. Retail trade thus lost its stigma among businessmen; wholesalers like the Findlaters through their wholesale interest in tea and spirits eventually opened a chain of retail shops; the Pims opened one of the first department stores in Dublin; the milling circle of Johnston, Mooney & O'Brien moved into baking and retail distribution. Shipowners began to emerge in their own right selling a service to a wide number of traders instead of being as in the past the poor cousins of the merchant and largely dependent for business on his goodwill. Insurance also began to emerge as a business in its own right, no longer dominated as in the past by merchants nor managed, as the first corporate ventures had been, by merchants. The merchant had been a single man with many functions; now as specialisation developed the number of businessmen increased, each typically exercising a sole function. These changes were reflected in the Chamber of Commerce, especially in the business functions of its prominent figures and in its membership at large. As the number of traders increased, professional men too had a wider circle of trade customers, were less overshadowed by the lordly figure of the great merchant, and were drawn towards the milieu of businessmen in the hope of picking up custom. Solicitors in particular began to be accepted into the Chamber in the 1860s and 1870s. The fall in membership (from 619 in 1832 to 543 in 1850) was reversed. In the late 1860s and early 1870s new members were admitted in large numbers and the fact that a number were refused, or were accepted after an initial refusal, illustrates the uncertainty which members of the Chamber at first experienced in widening the membership. By 1882 its membership had doubled from the low and declining figure of the early 1850s to 1180.

Even in the 1870s, the presidency of William Digges La Touche, though he was from one of Dublin's oldest financial families represented something of a change and of a reaching out to new frontiers. He had sold out the venerable La Touche private bank to the Munster, the newest and most thrusting of the Irish banks, and had accepted a directorship in return. He also held directorships in transport concerns — the Grand Canal Company and the Great Northern Railway — and thus anticipated a growing characteristic of the final decades of the century: the close interpenetration of banking and transport, which before this had only been evident in the Quaker links between the Royal Bank and the Dublin & Kingstown Railway. By the 1880s this interpenetration of interests was very marked. The Pims, for instance, were now represented both on the Grand Canal Company and on the Great Northern and Great Southern & Western railways, and their representation in these conservative bastions also led them onto the Board of the Bank of Ireland. In 1880 J. W. Murland, who was chairman of the Royal, was chairman of the Great Northern and vice-chairman of the G.S.W.R.; James Chaigneau Colvill, maintaining the Colvill tradition of prominence in the Chamber of Commerce had been governor of the Bank in 1870-73 and was chairman of the G.S.W.R. in 1880. The cross-channel shipping interests, once relatively minor, were growing rapidly and in the last two decades their prominence in the Dublin business world increased enormously. Through the Murphy, Martin and Kinahan families, the shipping interests were represented on the boards of the Hibernian, Royal and Bank of Ireland.

Again the cross-channel shipping interest overlapped into railways. The shipping Murphys (not to be confused with William Martin Murphy coopted in 1906) were aleady on the board of the Dublin Wicklow & Wexford Railway by 1880 and in 1891 the Cairnes involvement in the City of Dublin Steamship Company linked the steamship group with the Great Northern. The steamship interests were a very tight circle who were represented on the Irish Steamship Association. In conjunction with some of the railway interests they were responsible for the opening in 1891 of the City of Dublin Junction Railway which, in providing a link across the Liffey between the railway systems on both sides, was to rail transit what Butt Bridge had been twenty years previously to roads. The Dublin United Tramway Company represented the final stage in this circle of transport interests. William Martin Murphy was a contractor for many of the light railways in the 1890s, and in the classic pattern of a railway promoter he and his allies, several of them fellow-directors of the Dublin United Tramway Company, provided some of the capital and became directors of the companies. In subsequent years the pattern of directorships also illustrates a very close link between Murphy and the Hibernian Bank. The Hibernian had associations with the Dockrell family who were directors by 1902: significantly, though members of the Church of Ireland and unionists, the Dockrell link with the nationalist circle around the Hibernian may explain why the family played an active role in the public life of the State after 1922.

Sir John Nutting, Bart., born in Bristol, England, 1852, was a director of the Dublin & Kingstown Railway and chairman of E. & J. Burke.

The Nutting and Kinahan family became prominent in the Dublin business community and in the Chamber in the 1860s or 1870s with the growth of Irish drink exports. The Nuttings were managing directors of the firm of E. & J. Burke, bottlers, bonders and warehousers of whiskey and stout, who had large premises in Dublin, Liverpool and New York. The Kinahans' business, originally a wine importing concern, was metamorphosised into a whiskey exporting business based on Dublin and London in the course of the nineteenth century. Thus in the second half of the century both houses were part of the far-flung business conducted from Dublin, Liverpool and London in stout and whiskey, highly specialised wholesalers whose role matched and indeed made possible the extensive distribution of two prestigious beverages. Emigration from both Ireland and Britain helped to diffuse taste for them, and few commodities from these islands can have been distributed more widely in the second half of the century than Guinness stout and Power and Jameson pot-still whiskey. Both families had close ties with the banking world, and the Kinahans in addition at one time or another held directorships in the Grand Canal Company, in the City of Dublin Steam Packet Company and in the City of Dublin Junction Railway Company.

This was still a tight business world with ties of family as well as of commerce running through it; but it was quite different from the old business world of the 1860s and earlier. It was characterised by two differences: first the emergence of close links between business and transport concerns, secondly the cessation of the Chamber's political role. As for the close links between business and transport concerns: no less than four directors of the Chamber of Commerce emerged between 1882 and 1920 from the steamship interests. Two other presidents, Wigham, and William Martin Murphy came

James F. Lombard, chairman, Dublin United Tramways, West and South Clare railways and Knight of the French Legion of Honour. He died in 1901.

from the circle centred upon the Dublin United Tramway Company. Thus what might be described loosely as the transport group provided six of the presidents of the Chamber of Commerce. Another four were importers, two of tea, one of builders' goods, and one of corn. As two, John Mooney and J. Malcolm Inglis, had flour milling interests, they can be regarded as importers because of the overwhelming importance of imported wheat in the industry. Of the remaining presidents, one was a cattle exporter, one a builder; only five were manufacturers, three of them in the closely related fields of brewing and malting. The Chamber was thus overwhelmingly commercial in the interests of its presidents. Some significant conflicts can be detected when discussion of controversial issues took place. Thus, when in 1902 the passionately discussed question of railway rates came up, there were, not surprisingly, defenders of the companies as well as critics. The question of free trade versus protection was also becoming controversial at the outset of the century. In 1903 at a special general meeting a resolution in favour of tariff reform was put forward by F. J. Usher, seconded by William (later Sir William) Goulding. An amendment, tabled to kill this resolution off, simply calling for a government inquiry was adopted 'by a large majority'. At the annual general meeting in 1904 the president told the members that the Council itself was divided on the issue. W. Field, at the annual general meeting in 1903, declared that 'the majority of the members were rather disposing of foreign manufactures than filled with an endeavour to encourage home and native industry'. The divide was not of course a simple one of traders versus manufacturers. Manufacturing interests catering for the home market held a different view from manufacturers with a large export base. When the issue came up again in 1910, a resolution was passed in favour of tariff reform (a polite word for protection). A letter from Sir William Goulding, the fertiliser manufacturer, stated that he favoured reform and that he thought that Ireland had lost more from free trade than other parts of the United Kingdom. Another resolution was put forward by G. N. Jacob, who said that he was a free trader, trying to put off the issue by calling for a study.

The rapid growth in membership in the 1860s and 1870s was bound to lead to change. The process was all the more inevitable as the structure of Dublin trade altered rapidly in the period from 1850 to 1876. In these years, with rising incomes in Ireland and lower transport costs, the traditional trade pattern of a large excess of exports was replaced by an emerging excess of imports. Thus, when the old pattern of presidency was broken by the election of a tea merchant in 1882, it was almost symbolic. The first sign of new vigour in the Chamber was in 1878 when a committee of 12 members was appointed by the annual general meeting to assist the Council in revising the rules. Most of the members of the Committee bore relatively new names which were to become prominent in the future history of the Chamber, and included Thomas Dockrell, James Fitzgerald Lombard and Thomas Martin. The moving spirit among them seems to have been Abraham Shackleton, a flour miller from Lucan with a Quaker background. The new resolutions were adopted at a special meeting later the same year. The most important was one that the Council should be increased to 27 members and that nine should fall to be elected every year. Elections took place in many years in the 1880s, even if there were few candidates offering themselves; and in two years when there were no

1

VALUE FOR CASH

This Splendid Suite in Figured Oak cannot be bought elsewhere in the Irish Free State at less than 17 guineas. You can buy it at Roches Stores for 13 Guineas, because here everything is sold for cash only at prices based on half the usual profits. It is made in Dublin workshops under our own supervision, and we know that it is substantial in every part, soundly built, and well finished.

Selling for Cash Only at **£13 13 0**

Roches Stores
CASH ONLY — HALF PROFITS
DUBLIN LTD.   HENRY STREET

And at Patrick St., Cork

3

Visitors to the Gordon-Bennett Race
WILL FIND
HIGH-CLASS ACCOMMODATION AND STRICTLY MODERATE CHARGES AT

ROOMS FOR 150 GUESTS

Electric Light Throughout ELEVATOR

JURY'S HOTEL, COLLEGE GREEN, DUBLIN.
Wires: "Jury." Phone, 503.   APPLY MANAGER.

1903

2

The
PERFECT CIGARETTE

The best that money can buy

These Cigarettes have a reputation for quality that has made them the choice of experienced smokers in Ireland and abroad.

CONTENTMENT IN EVERY PIPE
Cool, fragrant and satisfying—you'll know the real joy of smoking when you smoke

MICK McQUAID
CUT PLUG

Sweet Afton Cigarettes & Mick McQuaid Tobacco
ARE MANUFACTURED BY

P. J. Carroll & Co. Ltd., Dundalk, Irish Free State
Tobacco manufacturers for home and export trade
New York address : 100 Fifth Avenue. Canadian address : McIntyre Buildings, Victoria Square, Montreal

4

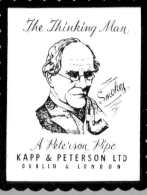

The Thinking Man Smokes

A Peterson Pipe
KAPP & PETERSON LTD
DUBLIN & LONDON

5

TYLERS' BOOTS ARE THE BEST

TONS SOLD WEEKLY IN THE TOWNS INDICATED

BRANCHES EVERYWHERE

That Tylers' Boots and Shoes are Best, Is known through North, South, East and West From Pole to Pole on every Sole Their Boots have firmly stood the test.

The Bright Spots of Ireland.

Abraham Shackleton,
photographed by
Lawrence of Dublin.

candidates beyond the number to fill the nine vacancies, 1881 and 1884, Shackleton forced a ballot by offering himself for election. The ballots he received — 153 in 1881 and 82 in 1884 — are almost certainly some measure of the 'radical' discontent in the Chamber.

The object of the ginger group of 1878 was clearly to force elections, but the proposals, though adopted, cannot have been to the liking of the essentially conservative Chamber because the pace of change remained slow. Shackleton in 1892 proposed the deletion of the paragraph on the 'state of trade' in the draft annual report of the Council as not reflecting the sentiments of the Chamber. This according to the minutes of the meeting was lost 'by a very large majority'. At the annual general meeting in 1895 Shackleton complained that he had failed, despite efforts, to get the annual report before the meeting. The secretary, Inglis, admitted the failure and the bland character of the Chamber comes across strikingly in the comments of the secretary:

> He took it as a good augury that that meeting was not by any means so crowded as they had seen on the occasion of former meetings. It was he thought a sign that things were going smoothly, just as when at a meeting of a public company it was considered a good sign if the attendance of shareholders was small.

The image of the Chamber was at this stage at a low ebb. Shackleton in 1897 congratulated the Chamber in a left-handed way on some action by a body 'which was considered conservative and narrow-minded — that had often been said about the Council and he might have said it himself'. Contested ballots appear to have been few in the 1890s, but if the challenge in the 1880s had not gained ground, the criticism was now more vocal than in the past.

What took place in 1870 was a changing of the guard. A new group of businessmen more closely related to the trades of the day and intimately connected with the transport and banking companies, became the dominant force. They were themselves a tightly-knit group, and no more than their predecessors did they have a serious interest in an opening up of the Chamber of Commerce. The paucity of ballots in the 1890s was one index of that, and the increase in the subscription in 1892 was interpreted by opponents as a proof as well. Their advent did however create one major change which was essential for the health of the Chamber: they broke the political link so that it was no longer part of the old unionist machine in the city. Even critics of the Chamber — and it had to bear some strong criticism from within and without in the 1890s — were prepared to concede this point. The nationalist M.P., William Field, who attended ex-officio as an M.P. for the city admitted in 1903 that 'no doubt, the Chamber was no longer looked on as a political institution, as it used to be'. Some of these businessmen, like George Kinahan who had been a supporter of Isaac Butt's home rule movement in the early 1870s, or the dominant group in the Royal Bank who had been liberal as opposed to conservative in their politics, had little in common with the old unionist group. The change in the personnel of the Chamber allied to the lack of ties with the old political machine of itself ensured the breakdown of its political complexion. At the same time it is true of course that, under the threat of land agitation and more extreme support for home rule, businessmen were as a whole drawing closer together in the 1880s, and the gulf that had existed between them as late as the early 1870s was less marked. Extreme nationalists were also beginning to express violently critical opinions of businessmen, and sweeping condemnations of businessmen themselves sometimes exaggerated the political complexion of the Chamber. A speaker at the annual general meeting in 1896 claimed that:

> The present High Sheriff of Dublin was boycotted and blackballed in that chamber not once but twice and three times. If so where was the ground for the honorary secretary to twit members for not coming in then. The High Sheriff had complained to him personally that he could not enter the Chamber. That fact alone was sufficient to show that there was a close chamber. Mr. Brown said that if they were to have a banquet of the citizens of Dublin, let it be a banquet of the citizens, and not a banquet of a Tory Chamber.

However, criticism now bore on the views of members themselves, not on the Chamber itself as a political institution. Whatever its failings, the Dublin Chamber was able to retain a façade of unity in contrast to the Cork Chamber which fractured into two bodies amid the political storms of the 1880s.

Criticism was somewhat exaggerated, but it drew strength from the history of membership. This had fallen continuously from a high point of 1180 in 1882 to 767 by 1899, and was attributed later to the raising of the subscription to £2 in 1892. The raising of the subscription had been a highly contentious issue and two conflicting resolutions were before the meeting in October 1892 which decided on the issue, corresponding to two interest groups in the Chamber, the anti-group predictably including Shackleton as seconder of its resolution. However, the subscription increase was overrated as a factor in the fall in membership. It was already falling before 1892, and the decline continued over the 1890s, so that the subscription cannot itself have been the main factor. The Chamber, in admitting a wider range of businessmen from the 1860s, may in fact have devalued its own prestige, a point hinted at in the explanation suggested by one of the Goodbodys in 1903 as a reason for the fall in membership: since companies had become limited liability companies, managers were reluctant to be seen by their shareholders. Much more damaging than the rise in subscription or some decline in the social standing of members was the cliquish image the Chamber created. While big businessmen were prepared to support the Chamber, many lesser members clearly were not, and voted with their feet. Though the membership was quite different from that of a quarter century previously, few if any elections were contested after 1887, and this picture of control would be still more

Insignia presented to the Dublin Chamber of Commerce by William Martin Murphy in 1913. Enamel on 18 carat gold by West & Son Ltd., Dublin.

80

striking if the Council domination of appointments to office was taken into account. An interesting conflict took place in 1884 at an annual general meeting over a proposal to move premises because 'they have been unable to free the Chamber from the evil influence caused by the licensed public-house called the *Bodega* in connection with these premises'. This proposal was lost by 51 votes to 133 and seems to have represented over a minor and possibly largely irrelevant matter a challenge to the Chamber's ruling establishment. Their victory was never to be forgiven them, and in 1903 a member in full-scale onslaught on the Council declared, according to a newspaper report, that:

> There was neither life nor soul in this body for years past ... Although he had no objection to a good glass of whiskey himself [laughter] he objected to see men oscillating between the rooms of that institution and the cellars of the basement. That was so years ago. He should feel gratified if the association could let the cellars downstairs to some Irishman who would carry on an Irish business. The *Bodega* was the tenant of the association ['no, no, you don't know what you are talking about'].

Sir James Murphy, Bart., born Dublin 1843, president of the Chamber, 1903-4, chairman of The Royal Bank of Ireland, consul for the Imperial German Empire.

Yet, despite and indeed because of criticism the Chamber was changing. Its elections were contested in 1901-1903, and although they were not contested again until 1910, the Council membership was more varied, and in particular the wide range of interests from which presidents were drawn reflected a much wider focus than in the past. Sir J. Malcolm Inglis, a director of the Royal Bank, president in 1900-1902 (who as secretary in 1895 had been so complacent about badly attended meetings) may have been the last president from the old school, to be succeeded by a succession of more vigorous presidents, only one of whom, Sir James Murphy in 1903-4, came from the dominant interest group of the Chamber in the preceding two decades. There was a good deal of discussion at meetings over the first decade, which suggests that it was becoming a more lively body on the floor, and at the annual general meeting in 1911 several members were critical of the absence of new blood. One member directly attacked the manner in which co-options between elections were operated, saying that it excluded the introduction of new members onto the Council except by doing so at the annual elections 'in the face of retiring members'. Some members were prepared to press for effective elections. A resolution requiring a ballot vote of the Chamber in Council elections came up in a meeting a month later in March, although it was not pressed to a vote, But there was some trenchant criticism, one member even describing the Council 'as the most amiable fossils'. This was perhaps a little less than cognisant of the changing realities, because the Chamber was strengthening over this decade., But the strong citicism was itself part of the new vigour, because the elections, which were contested in 1910 and 1911, were contested every year up to 1920. In contrast to the past the emphasis on recruitment had ceased to be the refrain of a minority to become one by the Council itself. In 1911 when the membership stood at 676, the Council report noted that 'the Chamber however is not as regards its membership proportionate to the mercantile position of the metropolis of Ireland'. The election of William Martin Murphy as president in 1912 and 1913 would thus seem to mark the culmination of a period of new vigour in

William Martin Murphy, born Bantry, Co. Cork, November 21, 1844. Built railways and tramways in Ireland, Britain and Africa. Nationalist MP for St. Patrick's, Dublin, 1885-1892. Founded the **Irish Independent,** *1905. President of the Chamber 1912-13. Died in Dublin, June 25, 1919.*

the Chamber's fortunes. The fall in membership from 759 in 1900 to 604 in 1909 was reversed, recovering to 680 in 1914.

Interestingly the Chamber's own interests were very much on his mind in his address at the annual general meeting in January 1913, and this was symbolised in his presentation to the Chamber of a chain of office for the president, a symbol which, in contrast to many other chambers, the Dublin Chamber lacked.

The novelty of Murphy's address, the most wide-ranging so far in the history of the Chamber, was heightened by his addressing himself to social issues. Commenting on the improvement in economic conditions in Dublin he observed:

> There is, however, another side to the picture when we come to consider the position of the working part of the population of our city, especially of the unskilled and consequently the lowest-paid workmen. The case of the farmers' prosperity — viz. high prices for their produce — means less food for the same money, or more money for the same food to the town labourer, who has to pay for everything he consumes, and has not even the potato patch or a cheap cottage which helps his country brother. A little more than a year ago we had a good deal of unrest amongst the unskilled workmen of Dublin, due in my judgment to the pinch of higher prices for the necessaries of life. Happily during the last year we have been comparatively free from these troubles, and I would exhort employers of labour not therefore to think that all was well and so neglect to consider with sympathy the conditions and wages of their employees, especially those in the lowest grade who are so seriously affected by any rise in the price of food.

He dwelt too on housing:

> The insanitary surroundings of the poorer classes in this city and the conditions under which they are obliged to live cannot and should not be, a matter of indifference to the commercial community. I am sure they are willing to bear their share in the cost of remedying this state of things, which is a stigma on this city . . .

He reminded tenement dwellers too that they had part of the remedy in their hands by exercising their votes discriminatingly at election time. His comments had been triggered off by the labour unrest in 1911, discussed in the Chamber in September 1911 when business had been dislocated by the railway strike, and when Murphy had cautioned wilder elements by reminding those who wanted a strong line with pickets taken by the authorities that an assembly of peaceful picketers could not be interfered with. The meeting proposed a small committee to consider the issue, and subsequently a meeting of employers of labour throughout Ireland, convened by the Council, was held in Dublin, and formed a representative committee to give effect to the resolution. This does not appear to have been successful, but it helped to prepare employers for a vigorous response in 1913.

Ironically, since Murphy had boasted in January 1913 that he had experienced no labour trouble in fifty years in business, his own empire was to be at the centre of that which started in Dublin in August 1913. The

Head of James Larkin, by Mina Carney.

trouble began in the Dublin United Tramway Company where Larkin and his Transport Workers' Union demanded an increase in wages, and widened alarmingly in the use by Larkin of the sympathetic strike both in Murphy's other enterprises and in business at large which had dealings with Murphy's companies It thus took on the proportions of a major confrontation, and Murphy took the step of locking out any workers who refused to sign an undertaking not to become members of Larkin's union.

From the trams the dispute first spread to the *Irish Independent,* and from that newspaper to Easons, the news wholesalers who distributed it, soon affecting much of the port business and economic life of the city. At a meeting of the Chamber on 1 September 1913 a resolution was passed congratulating Murphy on the stand he had taken in his business. Murphy set out his own position in a fighting manner at the meeting:

> He had seen for a long time that the head of this labour agitation in Dublin has been aiming for a position that was occupied some time ago in Paris by a man who was called 'King' Pataud who was able to hold up the whole business of the city by raising his little finger. That man was driven out of Paris, and the other would be driven out of Dublin shortly. The question he fought in connection with the Tramway Company was not one of wages or treatment of those employed in the tramway service. The whole issue was whether Mr. Larkin was going to rule the trade of Dublin . . . The position was becoming intolerable. It was time to stop this man and (said Mr. Murphy) 'I think I have stopped him'.

Murphy expressed a wish to have an employers' association formed, and the resistance to Larkin was conducted through the committee of this association. Not all employers, however, took an equally hard line, and the issue surfaced at a Council meeting on 27 November when with a general meeting in prospect for 1 December two resolutions were before the Council, one supporting Murphy's hard-line and the Employers' Executive Committee, the other while condemning the sympathetic strike stating that the employers should withdraw the undertaking which workers were required to sign as an infringement of workers' personal liberty.

It was decided not to press the resolutions to a vote, and this decision may have been influenced by a very strong letter from Sir William Goulding requesting the withdrawal of both resolutions 'as I consider that it would at the present critical time cause a great deal of ill-feeling and division in the Chamber which I think would be more harmful to the interests of the employers'. Thus the labour trouble passed the Chamber over at least publicly. It had, however, contributed to making 1913 an unprecedently busy year. There were no less than 50 meetings of the Council, but the large number was in the main due to a rise in the general level of activity of the invigorated Chamber.

The conflict was referred to only briefly in the annual report for 1913, and at the annual meeting in January 1914 Murphy, completing his second year as president, simply referred to 'the utter failure of the syndicalist system'. He even stated 'that the victory they had won should not, however, absolve employers from the obligation of seeing that their work force receive

a wage which will enable them to live at least in frugal comfort'. But the discord over the methods pursued in the strike did surface at the meeting. There was one dissenting voice on the adoption of the report: that of James Brady, a solicitor who maintained that there were faults on both sides, and that it had been characterised by a clash of personalities. There is no doubt that Murphy, despite some differences of opinion, had a solid majority behind him. The Chamber commissioned a portrait by Orpen in 1914, and when he came up for election again in January 1917 he headed the ballot. In fairness to the Chamber, which supported a hard line, it did not, in what the Council clearly regarded as victory, overlook the housing question. A resolution at a meeting in March 1914 unanimously supported immediate public action on housing and expressed its confidence that the ratepayers would support a sound, well-thought-out scheme. War overtook the matter, but at the annual meeting in January 1919 a resolution was passed calling on the government and treasury to subsidise the building of 18,000 cottages on 'virgin ground'. The proposer was Brady, and the seconder William Field. The initiative thus came from a minority group on the Council, but it passed nonetheless. At a Council meeting in May 1919, presided over by Murphy, the Council was asked by the Citizens' Housing League to appoint members to a deputation to wait on the Prime Minister and the leaders of the principal parties. Sir Horace Plunkett and Shanks were nominated by the Council. Later in 1919 the Council, in response to a request from the Dublin Housing Committee, repeated its view on the need for a national financial policy if the problem was to be remedied, and also stated that in addition to 'the admitted shortage of houses', 'there will probably be a further annual demand of not less than 500 houses arising from industrial expansion . . .'

Over four years the war dominated proceedings directly or indirectly and the Chamber identified itself solidly with the effort to win. Even before 1914, it had identified itself with the British armed forces. When the Lord Mayor had refused in 1913 to undertake the organisation of a presentation to H.M.S. *Dublin*, the Chamber took over the task. The Council in 1914 funded a motor ambulance at the front, and in 1915, at a special general meeting addressed by the British commander in Ireland, it unanimously adopted a resolution supporting recruitment. William Field was among the supporters, and according to the minutes the meeting ended with the singing of the national anthem. By October the secretary of the Council had negotiated with the military authorities the formation of a commercial company attached to the 5th Royal Dublin Fusiliers. The 1916 rebellion which caused so much destruction in the city was scarcely reflected in the proceedings at general meetings at all. In May, the president for 1916 referred, according to the minutes, 'to the unfortunate disturbances which had recently occurred'. At a special meeting on 5 May, on the other hand, the Council assured the king of the loyalty of the commercial community. It attributed the rebellion to the 'gross laxity' of the Irish administration. However, when it called for an enquiry into the methods and procedures of the Irish administration ten days later the strong language of Sir William Fry who proposed that 'the control of affairs in Ireland should be best in the hands of the military authorities until the rebellion was stamped out and the leaders thereof brought to justice' did not find favour with it, and more moderately it sought that

Sir William Goulding, Bart., chairman of W. & H. M. Goulding and of the Great Southern and Western Railway; High Sheriff of Dublin 1906 and of Co. Kildare 1907.

William Fry, JP, born Dublin, June 10, 1853, partner in the firm of William Fry and Son, solicitors and land agents; according to **Contemporary Biographies** *(1908) "finds recreation in visiting parts of the world not overrun with tourists".*

'military control of the city should be maintained in an efficient form until the public safety is assured and the civil administration is reconstituted on an efficient basis'. In February 1917 a special general meeting was called to support the war loan, and a resolution to that effect was passed unanimously. The only note of dissent from government policy was heard in 1917 at an extraordinary general meeting called to consider the effects of government restrictions on malting,. brewing and distilling. This was a measure on which an Irish Chamber was bound to find common accord. There were only three dissentient voices, those of Joseph Mooney, Grierson and Charles Eason who seem to have represented a temperance view. However, the changing temper of the times was beginning to be reflected in the Chamber, at least from the time that conscription was proposed in 1918. At an extraordinary meeting in June 1918 a resolution was proposed 'that it is inopportune at the present time for the Council of this Chamber to present any address of welcome to his Excellency the Lord Lieutenant'. The resolution was proposed by Foster Carton, a Smithfield salesmaster, and seconded by Patrick Leonard, also a salesmaster who had been president in 1915. It was a heated meeting: both men according to the minutes spoke 'at considerable length', and the proceedings were forced to a conclusion only by proposing that the question be put. The resolution was finally lost by what is described in the minutes as 'a large majority'. However, even if a political division had shown itself in the Chamber, radicalism was a feature of fringe groups represented by a professional man like Brady or, as with Carton and Leonard, individuals involved in an activity close to the temper of rural Ireland which was conspicuously less enthusiastic than the towns in war loyalty and fervour for the Crown. Even at the meeting on the special loan in 1917, a tone of disapproval of the farming community was evident with criticism being expressed by several prominent members of the prosperity of the farmers and their lack of readiness to take money out of bank deposits and put it into government loans. At an extraordinary general meeting in July, addressed by the Recruiting Council for Ireland, the president was able to welcome its members 'who were carrying out a most patriotic work' and to assure them 'of the hearty support of the Chamber'. In October a unaminous resolution of congratulations to General Foch was passed.

Superficially the Chamber survived the war unscathed. But in fact it changed considerably, and its prominent new members were different in many respects from the old guard. Moreover, the impressive unanimity was in part due to the support of the nationalists for the war effort. The old generation of nationalists still supported voluntary recruitment in 1918, even if rural Ireland was now being alienated at a pace the rapidity of which few realised at the time. The chief address at a special meeting on recruiting in July 1918, a moving one, was by Captain Gwynn, a nationalist M.P. There was a real difference, however, in sentiment between many of those who supported a resolution in favour of the Navy at a Council meeting in August 1915 and its proposer Sir William Fry who could speak of 'our country' and 'our empire'. And this gulf could only widen as war in Ireland and questions of self-government came to the fore in 1919 and 1920. Moreover, the political divide grew because the Chamber itself was changing significantly in composition in the 1910s. This was already happening in the first decade of the century, and its pace accelerated in the second decade. New articles of association were adopted in 1914. One of them stated that the presidency should be held for only a year at a time, a reflection of a democratic wish to have a more representative direction of the Chamber. The results were highly significant. Of the first six presidents elected under the new rules, only two Andrews (tea, 1918) and Wallace (steamships, 1919) came from the old interest groups and neither came from families which had been prominent in the congerie of dominant directorships in Dublin banking and transport concerns. Wallace and Hewat, a post-1920 president who also became a very active member at this time, were both coal importers who integrated backwards into shipping: they did not really spring from the cross-channel milieu, a fact very evident in the discussion in 1901 on the thorny question of whether the Port and Dock Board's revenue should derive from dues on tonnage or on goods. Patrick Leonard, the first of the presidents under the new articles, in 1915, came from the socially lower group of cattle salesmasters, and like Minch in 1917 (a maltster), represented activities more closely related to agricultural Ireland than to the city. In 1920, a builder, John Good was elected. None of these men were prominent in the world of interlocking directorships in banks and transport companies. This change was reflected too in the elections to the Council: not only were new faces emerging but they were coming out of different interest groups and more miscellaneous activities, and some prominent businessmen who, though members, had traditionally stood aside from the Chamber's activities were now playing a more active role. Charles Eason, who had rarely attended, was also now

The Year Book for 1917 published by the Chamber contained a page of adhesive stamps for affixing to letters advocating the commercial advantages of Dublin.

becoming a participant in meetings. In February 1918 he spoke on a resolution requesting the appointment of a commission of enquiry into local government in Dublin borough. The passing of the resolution was itself significant. The old Chamber, largely made up of men living in the security of the independent townships, had been anxious to avoid local government issues because of the implications of redrawing boundaries. Indeed Andrew Jameson was the only member of the old family and business group with the mental flexibility to appreciate the inevitability of change. Thus in March 1918 Good's proposal of new articles of association was supported by Jameson, although they were not adopted because they did not get a three-quarters majority. In 1917 a member of the Jacob family, who had conspicuously avoided involvement in public life, was elected to the Council for the first time. Jacob was a very close acquaintence of Eason's, and both in turn were close to William Martin Murphy's family. Lombard Murphy, like Eason and Jacob, was to be prominent in the Chamber in the 1920s. Significantly, the changing composition of the Chamber also corresponded to a divergence from the interests of the financial group. At the special meeting in 1917, the criticism of farmers would hardly have been shared by bankers who benefitted from farmers' deposits and in 1918 the Chamber even had an address on the subject of 'how our banking system restricts trade'. Banking had, in fact, been changing rapidly in the late nineteenth century. Until the 1870s advances equalled deposits; the consequence was that banking was closely geared to trade activities, and directors often had business interests. After the 1870s, advances began to fall progressively short of deposits (a trend not confined to Irish banking), and investment on the London money market began to absorb much of the resources of the banks. This broke the close link with trade and industry; fewer directors had business interests or were businessmen, and as the interlocking character of business, transport and banking began to weaken, the harmony between the three sectors was less assured than formerly. Banking was now dominated more by self-perpetuating financial interests such as the Colvills who had finally in the late nineteenth century severed their century-old ties with trade and industry. The Hibernian, long a 'non-conformist' bank politically, and latterly in banking practice, was the most immune to these tendencies.

The changes also reflected a desire for a more effective Chamber of Commerce. This was already evident at the end of the century in the organisation of addresses by outsiders on subjects of interest to businessmen. These were often fairly general though they included figures as famous as Gordon Selfridge. By 1917 the Chamber's talks had taken a very specific, practical turn. In that year there were talks both on the sugar beet industry and on industrial alcohol. The Council also took a keen interest in commercial education. The poor showing of Irish candidates in the London Chamber of Commerce examinations was a factor which led it to campaign vigorously in 1908 for Commerce as a subject in the National University of Ireland, and in 1913 to press for night teaching. Even under the shadow of war the Chamber planned to bring out a year book. It had on several occasions in the past been berated for the failure to produce any publication other than the annual report. The year book appeared in 1917. It was an attractive publication with much information on the city and the history of

11

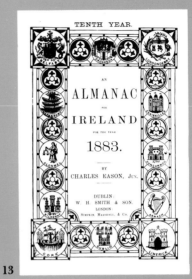

13

INVOICE. 39460

PHONE 1453.

124 & 125 CAPEL STREET.

Dublin, 1/3/27 19

Bought of THOMAS LENEHAN & CO.,

Manufacturing Smiths, Ironmongers and Implement Merchants.

ALL KINDS OF FARM MACHINERY.

Interest charged on overdue accounts at Bank Rate.

12

14

its industries as well as practical information. The directory section was printed in four languages reflecting the interest in obtaining markets abroad, and a novel detail, derived from the new alertness of the Chamber, was that Russian was one of the four languages. Underneath the facade of imperturbability suggested by the unanimous or near-unanimous public face the Chamber maintained, there was evidence of real change and of vitality. These qualities were to give it the resilience which enabled it to absorb the sweeping political and economic changes which were now about to overtake the country.

─────────── VII ───────────

The new State
*1920*1939*

The Chamber of Commerce had changed considerably in the second decade of the century. Its membership had changed a good deal too, and in particular many of its officers were now either Catholic or Protestant businessmen who were not prominently identified with the old establishment. All this was to give the Chamber some flexibility of outlook, which meant that it could cope relatively readily with the changes which were now about to affect the political and economic environment. Families like the Dockrells and the Goods, for instance, had no close associations with the older business establishment, and hence were ready to play a part in the public life of the new state. Thus John Good, who had been president in 1920, was to become a T.D. in the new order, and more strikingly the Dockrells, who had late come to prominence in the Chamber before 1920 and one of whom was a unionist member of parliament, were to continue a close association with the Chamber and with public life. H. M. Dockrell was to become a T.D. and in 1933 was to be president of the Chamber. Its presidents over the 1920s were to be a mix of Protestants and Catholics, but with the exception of David Barry of the B. & I. and Senator Sir Walter Nugent, a bank and railway director, in 1928 and 1929 respectively, they were all or almost all from relatively new business families or from newer businesses.

As part of the change that was taking place, some families like the Easons and the Jacobs which had had no part in the activities of the Chamber began to play a prominent role. Such families, Dissenter like the Easons, Quaker like the Jacobs, had stood aside conspicuously from the city's business establishment. Charles Eason rarely attended and rarely spoke except on purely intellectual issues, but his son, J. C. M. Eason, who became a member in 1918 was to play a very active role in the Chamber and to become its first honorary member in later years. George N. Jacob was already active in the late 1910s and was to remain an active member throughout the 1920s. The link between William Martin Murphy, Charles Eason and George Jacob had developed at the time of the problems posed by the 1913 strike, and this group, embracing forceful Catholics and Dissenters, was to provide a cohesive centre group in the 1920s. Significantly, William Martin Murphy's son, Lombard Murphy, who had been coopted to the Chamber in 1919 on the death of his father, was president in 1924, followed by George N. Jacob two years later in 1926, and J. C. M. Eason in 1927. This group could, of course, have carried only a weakened or divided Chamber with them if they could not count on the backing of older and more conspicuously establishment business in the city. The election of Andrew Jameson as president for the

J. C. M. Eason, President 1927.

disturbed and crucially significant year of 1921 seems to have reflected a concern among members to find common ground in face of the many and menacing problems of the time. Jameson was one of the handful of prominent Protestant leaders who were keen on bridging the gap between nationalists and unionists, and enthusiastic that unionists should play a part in the public life of the new state. Significantly too, Bryan Cooper, the head of the Sligo landed family, who like Jameson believed in the active participation of Protestants in public life and was to be a T.D. in the 1920s, was a member of the Chamber between 1923 and his death in 1930. No less than nine members, appointed or elected to the Senate, were members of the Chamber, and the alliance of the Murphy-Jacob-Eason group and the Jameson group seems to have been the basis for the successful and relatively willing adaptation of the Chamber to the circumstances of the 1920s.

This was not as easy or as inevitable a result as might appear, reading back later from the relatively successful outcome. The problems of the Chamber were many, the one of most immediate concern being the economic situation. The report for 1919 could enthuse that 'Ireland during the past year has been again exceedingly prosperous'. That for 1920, on the other hand, had to note that 'trade during the earlier part of the year was on the whole good, but in recent months there has been a serious set-back, and it is now bad'. In appraising the outlook of businessmen, it must be remembered that throughout the first half of the twenties, they were having to adjust to novel political conditions in the midst of acute business depression. The first report again expressing optimism on the general economic front was that for 1927. It was this dismal situation, much more than doctrinaire grounds, that explains the repeated concern of the Chamber and its Council with the burden of taxes and rates, the need for economy in public services, and a reduction in public expenditure. A sign of the difficult times too was the fact that after a significant rise in the 1910s, membership continued to fall through these years.

The coincidence of a downturn in economic activity in 1920 with a worsening in law and order made the political situation in Ireland profoundly disturbing, and also made the uncertainties of novel political arrangements all the more unsettling. In 1919 on the occasion of the murder of Sergeant Barton in College Street, the Council declared that it 'feels that the time has now arrived when it is the duty of all classes to express their indignation at such cowardly and inhuman acts which are doing such incalculable injury to our city and country'. While the Chamber had hoped that things would get better, they actually deteriorated. The following year the annual report, submitted in January 1921, noted that 'this Chamber has not been lacking in its condemnation of these uncivilised and immoral happenings, and in recent months other bodies and important personages have uttered their denunciation, but the state of terror existing has precluded a whole-hearted and concerted protest from responsible bodies whose duty it is to speak out and thus do their part in an endeavour to bring to an end the terror that is rapidly destroying the trade of the country'.

Much of the Chamber's time in 1920 was taken up with the Government of Ireland bill: it appointed a committee which included members as varied in opinion as Richard K. Gamble (of Brook Thomas), Sir Horace Plunkett, W.

Lombard Murphy and Patrick Leonard to consider it. The committee and the sub-committee it in turn appointed met no less than 23 times in all. Its findings expressed apprehensions both about the effects of partition on trade and the costs of duplication of administrative machinery. The ultimate sense of the Council's resolution was contradictory: it supported a measure of self-government for Ireland while accepting that Ulster should no be coerced. Something of the unionist fear crept into its observation that partition would deprive the southern parliament of 'the steadying influence and business training of the men of Ulster, which would be a valuable asset in the moulding of legislation as well as in the guidance of the government of Ireland'. The Committee also disliked the fiscal conditions of the bill as 'the southern Irish parliament, while denied really effective control over large areas of Irish affairs, would be compelled to submit to taxation suited to British and not to Irish conditions'.

G. N. Jacob, President 1926.

The Council again condemned both the crimes and reprisals, but its report for 1920 could only note without hope that 'the lead given by your Council has been followed by leading men throughout the country, who have fearlessly voiced their views, but, unfortunately, so far no improvement has taken place'. The peace treaty signed a year later in December 1921 at last held out hopes and the Council passed a resolution that 'rejection of the Peace Treaty, and a return to chaos and civil war, with its untold miseries, as an alternative to acceptance [would be] unthinkable'. During the negotiations, in July 1921, the British side had put forward as one of its proposals a proposal ('no. 5') that the two governments should agree that no protective duties or other restrictions should be imposed upon the flow of goods between the two countries. The Chamber however was quick to point out that this was less equal than it seemed and that:

> An Irish parliament, under this condition, would find it impossible to follow the example of the Parliament at Westminster in passing an act for safeguarding of new or struggling industries which might become a great national asset. Ireland would also be bound, in advance, to a British trade policy without regard to its adaptability to the circumstances or conditions of the country.

In the event this clause did not appear in the final agreement.

The Chamber's hopes for an improved general situation were again dashed as civil war broke out in 1922. Even before the war began, the issue was casting a shadow over the Chamber's proceedings. In March a national fund called the 'Treaty Fund' was opened to meet the election expenses of Free State candidates. It was suggested that a subscription list for this Fund be opened in the Chamber of Commerce. The Council held a special meeting on the subject, but while recognising the need for 'a strong, settled government', it decided in line with its past policy of avoiding expressions of opinion on political issues that 'any action by the Chamber that would appear to take sides in the impending context would establish a precedent that might be harmful to its future welfare'. In April, as law and order began to break down, a general meeting of the Chamber called for the establishment of conditions of security and tranquility. Some suggestions were made that the Chamber itself should take part in the forthcoming general election either by way of nominating candidates or supporting

15

17

The Port of Dublin

Transit Sheds on North Quay, showing Railway Sidings.

Three Miles of Berthage with varying depths of water up to 32 feet.

Modern facilities for discharging and loading.

Sheds for accommodation of goods in transit with a cubic capacity of 2,300,000 feet. Goods lie in sheds for 7 days free.

Direct Rail and Canal communication with all parts of Ireland.

Ample Warehouse accommodation, including Cold Storage.

Sites for Factories with deepwater frontage and railway connections.

Full particulars can be had from

THE SECRETARY, Dublin Port and Docks Board,
19 Westmoreland Street, Dublin.

candidates in the commercial interest. Already in 1920 the Council, in regretting the loss of Northern businessmen, had expressed the view that a strong representation of businessmen in the southern parliament was necessary. The suggestions were referred to the Council which decided that even the exceptional conditions prevailing in 1922 did not warrant a departure from the policy of non-interference in politics. However, when the civil war was over, the Chamber took a more direct interest in the matter. In 1923, in anticipation of an approaching general election, a number of members, acting under the auspices of the Council, formed themselves into a Businessmen's Committee, in the words of the annual report, 'to secure the return to the Dail of candidates who would effectively represent business interests, which had hitherto been entirely unrepresented'. John Good and William Hewat (of Heitons), both former presidents of the Chamber, were returned for Dublin county and Dublin city north respectively. This may have helped both in gaining the acquiescence of members in the political changes, and in making it possible to put forward representations more effectively about matters of concern to the Chamber.

John Good, TD, President 1920.

Well before a separate parliament had emerged, the Council in its report for 1919, had occasion to complain that 'bill after bill, with lightning-like rapidity, has been introduced into parliament — indeed, there have been so many measures that it has been next to impossible for the businessmen of the country to keep pace with them . . . it has been found necessary to protest against the unseemly haste, which has not allowed of adequate consideration being devoted to proposals, in many cases involving vital issues'. This was not in itself a novelty; the point had even been made on the eve of the first world war, and the activity of the Chamber had risen to unprecedented levels at that time. The pattern was to be repeated in the post-war years. In 1919 there were 26 council meetings, and the year's president had to attend 43 meetings of committees. In 1920, when business was further swollen by the Government of Ireland bill, there were 17 council meetings but the number of other meetings over which the president was due to preside had risen to 80. In 1919 the number of committees had risen to eight. The creation of the Free State meant, of course, that the intense legislative process which might have been expected to ease off acquired a new impetus. As early as the general meeting of 25 October 1922, J. C. M. Eason, now one of the rising stars of the Chamber, stressed the importance of organisation if commercial interests were to receive attention in future and he supported the idea of creating an Association of Irish Chambers of Commerce, an idea mooted by the Council. The most critical single business issue affecting the Chamber was the proposed amalgamation of railways. The report for 1923 conceded that 'no more vital question confronts the country at the present time'. The Chamber had several links with the railway companies and the 1924 president, Lombard Murphy, was a director of one of them. The Railways bill which the government had introduced was denounced as creating 'a railway monopoly' and as being calculated to lead to nationalisation. Only three members dissented from the strong views of the resolution at the Chamber's extraordinary meeting in April 1924, one of them being James Brady who as always took the advanced line, this time favouring nationalisation. This issue threatened the emerging good relationship between the Chamber and the new government. Good was requested to table a number of amendments by the Council. According to the Council report for 1924 'all opposition to the Bill was met with "ridicule, abuse, and misrepresentation", and the bill was passed practically as introduced'. The Chamber's role which was deliberately intended to put off the legislation was attacked by the president of the Executive Council, W. T. Cosgrave, in the Dail on 11 April in strong terms:

> If there is one class in this community more responsible for the disorder that has taken place during the last two years it is the so-called businessmen.

This in turn led the Council to make its own formal protest 'in the strongest possible manner against the wholly unwarranted statement made by President Cosgrave'.

However, the relationship survived this strain, and it became closer as time went by. The Free State government was in fact anxious to make close contact with the Chamber. The report for 1922 had already noted that 'several of the Government departments have approached the Chamber for information and advice, which have in all cases been readily and promptly given, and the Government has been assured that the Chamber will be only too pleased to cooperate with any of the Departments in every way possible'. In1924, at the first general meeting of the new Association of Chambers of Commerce, which was intended to be a pressure group, the Minister for Industry and Commerce, Mr. McGilligan, gave an address and indicated that 'the Government would welcome a closer interchange of ideas with Chambers of Commerce'. This was in June, two months after the damaging Dail proceedings on the Railway bill, and was clearly an effort on both sides to mend fences. In the past the Chamber had had little direct contact with ministers. Apart from the banquet in 1769 for the Lord Lieutenant on the occasion of the laying of the first stone of the Royal Exchange, the first occasion on which a Lord Lieutenant was received by the Chamber at large seems to have been the visit to the Chamber of Lord Aberdeen in 1911. In October 1924 the Minister for Finance, Ernest Blythe, addressed the Chamber at an ordinary general meeting, the first of a pattern of frequent direct contacts which have been the practice ever since.

These new contacts, informal as much as formal, were also a means of defusing misunderstanding. There was a sharp contrast between the handling of the new legislation for electricity supply and the Railway bill. This issue was every bit as serious in its implications as railway amalgamation, and even more so as it actually introduced nationalisation, the proposed legislation providing for the taking over of existing undertakings. Hence it was in reality the crucial test of relationships between relatively conservative businessmen, many of them still doubtful of the State politically as well as economically and a government still feeling its way uncertainly amid the complex problems of the post-war world. When the Shannon scheme was first mooted, the views of the Council were that the government was pressing the scheme unduly in 1925, and the two Chamber of Commerce members in the Dail sought to seek further time for discussion 'without success'. It was thus shaping up for a further conflict of interest between the two sides and on the fundamental and emotive issues of

The Shannon scheme under construction. In 1931 W. D. & H. O. Wills issued a series of 40 cigarette cards describing the development.

CONSTRUCTION OF THE POWER STATION (A)

CONSTRUCTION OF THE PENSTOCKS (A)

nationalisation. In contrast to the railway issue, however, differences were softened by contacts outside the Dail chamber. The Minister for Industry and Commerce received a deputation, and attended the May meeting of the Chamber, making what the next annual report described as 'an excellent case for the scheme'. In fact the vote of thanks to McGilligan was passed 'with acclamation'. On the ever contentious question of postal and telephone rates, the minister, J. J. Walsh, met the Chamber in October 1925. In 1926 President Cosgrave himself accepted an invitation to address the Chamber, and when he was unable to attend because of illness, a message of sympathy wishing him a speedy recovery was sent. At the October meeting the president laid an emphasis on cooperation and in particular on the wishes of the business community to be consulted before bills were actually introduced into the Dail. The climate in which the matter was pursued, however, was now one of relative optimism, and J. C. M. Eason, the vice-president, stressed that he felt 'that the Chamber's voice was getting a more attentive hearing than was the case some time ago'.

It was in this new and less contentious climate that the actual setting up of the Electricity Supply Board came to be faced in 1927, a potentially explosive issue because it involved not simply the execution as in the case of the Shannon Scheme of an ambitious engineering project but the setting up of a body which would take over existing generating enterprises. It thus went beyond rationalisation as in the case of the railways to the provision of power to take into public ownership existing undertakings. While this issue was devoid of the political uncertainties of the first contacts between Chamber and government in 1922, it was a more direct confrontation of the issue which for conservatives heralded, along with strikes, the arrival of Armageddon. As the report for 1927 put it: 'probably no legislative measure in recent years excited so much comment and heated discussion among the general public . . . particularly in regard to the proposals that the Electricity Supply Board should be placed in a position to take over existing municipal electrical undertakings without compensation'. The issue was debated at no less than four special general meetings of the Chamber in 1927. The tone for the year was set by the fact that President Cosgrave's visit and address at last took place at the annual general meeting in January. As far as the Chamber was concerned the wider issue was also intertwined with the more practical one of electricity rates and of keeping them at a sufficiently high level to leave a surplus to apply to the reduction of the municipal rate. To make the Shannon Scheme a success it was essential that electricity rates should be low in order to maximise consumption, while Dublin businessmen with the city's own undertakings fully extended were more concerned with keeping rates sufficiently high to generate a surplus. At the first of the meetings a resolution was before the meeting opposing the measure, and its seconder, the influential and moderate George N. Jacob, even described the measure as 'legalised robbery'. Mr. McGilligan attended the second meeting. The minister went a long way towards meeting them on some of the points that concerned the Chamber, and the Chamber itself, while expressing a preference for allowing the existing undertakings in Dublin, Pembroke and Rathmines to continue under their existing management, conceded that there should be no contributions from the profits of the undertakings towards the relief of rates, in order that the price of current should be brought down to the lowest figure.

A minority of members proposed a resolution accepting the Shannon Scheme without any reservations at the meeting of 14 April. This would have had the effect not only of dividing the Chamber on a major issue but also of making the Council's own resolution appear more extreme than it was. The president, J. C. M. Eason, proposed a resolution which, while it expressed the Chamber's wish not to have the Dublin undertakings taken over, also contained a pledge for the Chamber 'to render all the assistance in their power to ensure the success of the scheme'. This resolution was passed unanimously, achieving thus a harmonisation between the government and the Chamber and between state intervention and the conservative stance of businessmen. In October 1928 the members of the Chamber visited the Shannon Scheme, in two express trains carrying in all a party of 500 with Mr. McGilligan as their guest. After the visit, the Chairman, D. Barry, stated that 'the Minister could rely on the members of the Chamber doing their best to make the Scheme a success. The visit to the Scheme, he said, had impressed the members of the Chamber with the importance of the undertaking'. Thus a scheme which could have left government and businessmen at daggers drawn had brought them into a new and closer relationship, and at the annual meeting in January 1928 John Mackie, one of the Chamber members sympathetic to the Shannon Scheme, could point to the 'friendly relations existing between the Government and the Chamber'. The president of the Executive Council, W. T. Cosgrave, paid his second visit to the Chamber in May 1928. David Barry, the year's president and a member of a family associated with the B. & I., was able to refer to 'the increased prestige of the State'. When the Minister for Agriculture met the members at the October meeting he was congratulated by Sir Walter Nugent 'on his very able speech and on what he had done for agriculture in the Free State'.

The active profile of the Chamber and the large issues of the 1920s ensured a reversal in the falling membership, which had declined to 678 at the beginning of 1924. In all 271 new members were elected in 1926, and the total at the end of the year had reached 882; 160 members were elected in 1927 and the total now reached 900. A high wastage rate reflected the high average age of members at the end of a period of falling membership.

At this stage, in October 1927, the Council introduced its Journal, apart

Senator Sir Walter Nugent, President 1929.

David Barry, President 1928.

THE SHANNON SCHEME.

A specially conducted tour for Members and their friends is being arranged for
WEDNESDAY, 3rd OCTOBER, 1928.
Special Train (1st Class) leaves Kingsbridge 9 a.m.
Tickets (including Light Luncheon, Dinner and Motor Conveyance at Limerick),

21/- each.

Number of tickets limited, and early application to the Chamber of Commerce is essential.

N.B.— The President Executive Council, the Minister for Industry and Commerce, and Members of the Electricity Supply Board have been invited as guests.

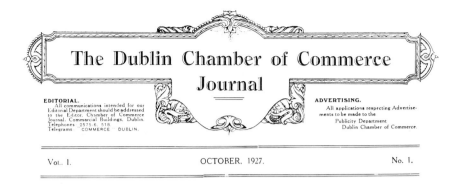

The Dublin Chamber of Commerce Journal

EDITORIAL.
All communications intended for our
Editorial Department should be addressed
to the Editor, Chamber of Commerce
Journal, Commercial Buildings, Dublin.
Telephones : 2575-6, 518.
Telegrams : "COMMERCE" DUBLIN.

ADVERTISING.
All applications respecting Advertise-
ments to be made to the
Publicity Department
Dublin Chamber of Commerce.

VOL. I.   OCTOBER. 1927.   No. 1.

from the Council's report its first regular publication which, with a free circulation, was intended to put Dublin business in contact with the outside world and to be the official organ of the Association of Chambers of Commerce. It was attractively laid out and ran a series of articles on Irish industries and on industrial history.

At the beginning of the 1920s the articles of association of the Chamber were changed to allow representation on the Council of nominees of companies or organisations. It was a measure of the standing of both Jamesons and Jacobs that they were the first two firms which came to be represented on the Council in that way. In 1923 both Andrew Jameson and George N. Jacob resigned their ordinary Council membership as they had been appointed to represent their companies. The Dublin Building Trades Employers Association was also represented in this way and in 1923 representation was also provided for the Irish Banks Standing Committee. The Dublin Stock Exchange and the Merchant Drapers Association of Dublin Limited also came to be represented on the Council under the new regulations.

A rise in membership in the 1920s accelerated the process of change in the outlook and character of the Chamber: indeed, even ahead of this its attitude was changing. A striking indication of this was the outlook on local government, which before the 1910s was one of opposition to change because it could only threaten the low-rated comfortable southern suburbs of the city. In the 1920s the Chamber vigorously attacked the inefficiency of the Corporation, the president James Shanks in 1923 at the May general meeting stating that 'there was not the smallest hope that the Municipal Council as at present constituted would attempt reform, and it would remain a blister on the civic life of Dublin until the citizens became sufficiently exasperated to make an end of it.' The Council in the shape of some of its new brooms, president Lombard Murphy, Eason, Crowe and Jacob, was represented at the local government enquiry into the administration of the affairs of Dublin in 1924. Eason made the case for the deputation, a scathing examination of the affairs of the Council. Before the subsequent Commission, Eason for the Council also made the case for the extension of the boundaries to cover the neighbouring townships. The wheel had now turned full circle: a new criterion of efficiency applied to both business and public administration overriding the narrow preoccupations of the past. So keen was the Chamber on the municipal issue that in 1930 in concert with the Dublin Mercantile Association it actually put up five candidates for the Dublin city elections, three members of the Chamber being elected: J. Hubbard Clark, Sir Thomas W. Robinson and C. E. McGloughlin.

The new vigour also applied to the Chamber's interest in education, where it continued its efforts to get Trinity College to introduce commerce as a subject. University College Dublin had already introduced commerce, and the Chamber had enjoyed close links with the professor, Charles Oldham. Even amid the preoccupations of 1920 the Chamber appointed an education committee including among others Sir Horace Plunkett, Lombard Murphy and John Good. While Trinity was prepared to create a school of Commerce, its proposals were less than satisfactory. The Committee requested that Good should appear before the Royal Commission on Dublin University, and the report for 1920 observed that 'any half-hearted measure which would have a tendency to make a student in the Faculty of Commerce feel inferior to his brother students in the professional Schools would be doomed to failure'. In 1921 John Good was appointed to a sub-committee within Trinity by the Board of the University. At length in 1925, to the great satisfaction of the Chamber, the University introduced its degree in commerce, and the Chamber exhorted employers to give preference to the graduates of the two Schools. The Chamber also took an interest in technical education, and when the government appointed a commission to advise upon a system of

technical education, the Council in 1927 submitted evidence to it. In 1930 a deputation headed by John Good discussed with the Department of Education the provisions of the Vocational Education Bill, and recommendéd that attendance at continuation schools should be made compulsory for young people, aged 14-16, not in approved employment. John Good, the member who had taken the keenest interest in education, left £5,000 in his will in 1941 to the Trinity College School of Commerce.

The 1920s represented a period of exceptional activity for the Chamber. In 1919 already there were no less than 26 council meetings and the number rarely fell below 20 in any year until the end of the 1920s. In 1920, while there were only 17 council meetings, the President could have presided over 80 committee meetings. The level was still very high until 1922. The year 1927, the year in which controversy over electricity supply reached its peak, repeated a similar pattern with 20 Council meetings and 63 other meetings. The utility of the Chamber as a body expressing the general voice of commercial interests rather than their sectional views was made very evident by some of the novel experiences of these years. Its role was marked in 1920 when a serious scarcity of coal developed because of the shortage of shipping. Its effects were so alarming that the Council appointed a special committee to deal with the matter. The Committee had great difficulty in getting statistics, and the president of the Chamber made several journeys to London to interview the Coal and Shipping Controllers. A promise was obtained from the Coal Controller to allocate 40,000 tons of coal per month from the South Wales fields. Notwithstanding this promise, in practice no coal was forthcoming. The Coal Controller alleged that it was because there was not adequate shipping available, while the Shipping Controller complained that the congestion was such that vessels often had to wait weeks at the South Wales ports before a turn at a loading berth. Eventually, the real causes were identified. Shipowners were shipping to continental rather than to home ports because in contrast to home freights the rates were not controlled. The Chamber after much difficulty persuaded the Shipping Controller to order a certain number of vessels to carry coal from South Wales to Ireland only, and priority of berthage was arranged for vessels in the coasting trade. In the matter of the mails also, in face of difficulties, Irish interests were treated in what the Council considered as 'a high-handed manner'. In the preceding year its utility had been proved in a threatened strike of bank officials, its intervention leading to a quick settlement of the dispute.

The Council was, of course, a conservative body in the matter of government regulation. In 1920 it observed that 'it is a strange thing that in every case where Government Control has taken place the trade and the public have equally suffered'. It was also very doubtful about the benefits of labour exchanges which it felt involved a large cost 'without offering anything like a commensurate return to employers or employees'. Its views on poor relief were also cautious: there was an interesting debate on the subject at a special general meeting in 1929. The members were unhappy about the charges that might fall on the ratepayers of Dublin, Pembroke and Rathmines, and while seeking to have any expenditure above a certain limit defrayed from central funds, they were opposed to an amendment which proposed that 'the burden is of a national character and should be carried by

19

21

20

22

*Sean Lemass, TD, (1899-
1971), Minister for
Industry & Commerce,
1932-1945, Taoiseach
1959-1966.*

the State'. One ex-president suggested that such an amendment would be 'disastrous as it might lead to poor relief all over the country becoming a national charge. Poor relief should be paid for in the area in which it was distributed'. The Chamber retained its interest in the housing question, although, overshadowed by more immediate political and economic issues, this had not surfaced much after the beginning of the 1920s. However, in 1930 the Chamber invited the Minister for Local Government to address the May general meeting, and a deputation also discussed the matter with the minister beforehand. Some of the concerns of the Chamber were reflected in a preliminary meeting of the deputation at which it was agreed that it was desirable that rent restrictions should be removed, subsidies stopped and steps taken to re-establish confidence in house-building as an investment. Discussion at the meeting, which was more general than usual, was inconclusive. While there was general agreement that more attention should be given to slum families compelled to live in one room and that the biggest problem was that of the slums, the members were clearly fearful of the implications of the extent of Local Government authority and were anxious to protect the role of private enterprise in house-building. The Minister himself had correctly anticipated the feeling of the members when in his address he put it that 'the question that had to be kept prominent was: who should build the houses for the worker earning £3 to £7 a week'. The Council report in 1931 stated that 'the big question to be settled is: Are local authorities to be the Landlords of the Working Classes'.

The optimism of the late 1920s on the economic front was maintained even into January 1930 when the Council submitted its annual report for 1929, observing that although 'the year has not fulfilled the promise of the spring, your Council believe that when the year's statistics are published they will show that progress has been made'. Even for the following year the report was able to say 'that members of the Chamber may find consolation in the fact that the Irish Free State is one of the countries which has been least affected by the prevailing depression'. In January 1932 the annual report expressed serious concern for the first time:

> In comparison with other countries the road upon which our State has travelled during the last few years has proved to be remarkably free from economic difficulties, but there are indications that new influences are developing which will materially affect our position, and call for alterations and adaptations in our internal economy.

At the general meeting in January in fact the policy conflicts of the future were anticipated. M. W. O'Reilly of the New Ireland Assurance Company declared that 'the Chamber should take first a purely Irish point of view and afterwards one in relation to world affairs and world economics'. He maintained that 'it was the duty of the Chamber of Commerce to give light to the people and indicate methods that might be adopted to put a stop to the false economic policy that was being followed'. This brought a rejoinder from J. C. M. Eason that 'there is no use being too dogmatic with regard to any course which the country should adopt', and that 'the policy of economic nationalism run mad' lay behind the troubles. The outbreak of the economic war with Britain in 1932 brought the issue into a practical realm more rapidly than any one might have expected. At the annual meeting of January 1933 the outgoing president, D. J. Cogan, stated that 'Your Council has repeatedly emphasised the importance of the British market to the farmers of this country and I do not think the experience of the past six months will lead to a change in its opinion'. However, if the government had critics, it also had defenders and M. W. O'Reilly declared that he did not approve of the report as there had been 'no suggestion of a constructive scheme or constructive thought on the subject of establishing national industries'. A reply to O'Reilly from David Barry, a leading figure in the Chamber, brought a rejoinder from T. J. Cullen that 'the present Government had done more to create employment for the people than the last Government had done in ten years'. However the views of O'Reilly and Cullen were those of a minority and the report was adopted.

Nevertheless the Chamber established a good relationship from the start with the new ministers. Sean Lemass, Minister for Industry and Commerce, addressed the Chamber in October 1933, and was well received. Sir Walter Nugent who proposed the vote of thanks said that 'the meeting struck a hopeful note', as 'it showed the good feeling which existed between the Minister and the commercial life of the country', and G. N. Jacob, who seconded, declared that the business community still felt that, whatever Government was in power, there was plenty of hope for Ireland, and instanced his own firm which he said had taken its 'courage in both hands, and had gone in for large extensions recently'. A meeting which the Minister for Finance attended in December 1933 was also cordial. In fact, many members benefitted from the policies which were introduced. The Chamber, heavily commercial in its composition in the past, seems to have shifted towards a larger representation of the manufacturing interest. A later analysis of the membership for 1937, allowing one or more occupations per member, suggested that Producers (41.6 per cent of the membership) equalled Commerce and Finance (42.6 per cent). Significantly, too, Miscellaneous Producers (15.0 per cent of the total membership) now outweighed the Makers of Food (12.1 per cent) which included very large firms and export-oriented industry. The report for 1934 was quite bland in its tone, and even conceded that the intensely disliked regulation of trade was 'necessary in the circumstances', and observed that 'in spite of the diminished earning power of agriculture revealed in the export figures, the members of the Chamber on the whole do not report a state of bad trade'. The address by the Chairman, H. M. Dockrell, T.D., at the annual meeting in January 1934 had already indicated an awareness that the burden had fallen on the farmers, observing that 'we have had from the Minister for Industry and Commerce a thorough exposition of the Government's industrial policy, but we have had no such complete and unified exposition of its agriculture, an omission which I think should be rectified at the earliest opportunity'. The continuing high level of economic activity in the towns, helped by a rise in real wages in industry and buoyant conditions in the construction industry, helped to blunt any criticism. In January 1936 the report noted that 'in Dublin during the year there has probably been an increase in the volume of trade'. It also noted that recent legislation regulating industry and commerce had increased the contact with

government departments and acknowledged 'the unfailing courtesy with which assistance has always been given by the officials of those departments'. Favourable comments on the government's policies were now becoming numerous, and J. Hubbard Clarke, outgoing president, in January 1936 declared that 'the Government deserves credit for much of this improvement and if they would settle the Economic War they have on with Great Britain they could solve many of the Free State's economic and financial problems in a very short time'. In fact an attitude of confidence was now beginning to develop. The financing of corporation housing schemes by loans was coming to be accepted, and Hubbard Clark declared that 'to my mind there is little use in preaching against Socialism and Communism so long as a great multitude of our fellow-citizens are compelled to live in hovels'. The Council's evidence submitted to the Dublin Housing Inquiry in 1939 illustrates this attitude very graphically. In fact, an atmosphere of complacency developed in the Chamber in the course of the 1930s. Despite the large amount of legislation and some critical comments on its implications, the Chamber had become markedly less active than in the 1920s. It failed to maintain publication of the attractive journal which it had launched in the late 1920s. The loss of members through age was not being compensated for, and by 1939 the membership, which had climbed to a high point in the 1920s, was down to a mere 601. In a decade in which the city's business grew and prospered on the Chamber's own admission, this was a singular phenomenon. It was clearly failing to attract new members, and reference to the increased use of regulation by ministerial order in an address by the president Hubbard Clarke in 1935 conveys something of the ineffective torpor which had descended on the Chamber:

> We endeavour to keep our members informed where Orders are made which affect them individually, but it is not possible to circulate information to all our members on every occasion. I, therefore, advise all members to pay frequent visits to the Chamber and to study the Notice Board.

While the complacent attitude helped to establish a good relationship between the Chamber and the Fianna Fail government and to secure acceptance by businessmen of novel and even controversial policies, it did not make for an active chamber and on balance can only have reduced the weight of the Chamber's voice.

An 1891 advertisement for The Bodega, a hostelry which was the cause of comment by members of the Chamber on several occasions (see pps. 81 and 109).

VIII

*'The Emergency' and the aftermath 1939*1983*

The Second World War was to create unique problems. The Chamber experienced a continuing decline in the early years: by January 1943 the membership had fallen to 544, the lowest level since the poor state of the Chamber's fortunes in the 1840s and 1850s. These were years in which there was sharp contraction in the city's economy following growth in output in several sectors in the 1930s. There was also, given the gravity of the crisis, unquestioned acceptance of draconian government regulation: in 1942 over 550 orders were made under various legislation. The nadir point in the economy was reached in 1943. Virtually every item was in short supply, and the report for that year noted 'continued hardship and difficult conditions for all, particularly for the poorer members of the community of this City'. The domestic ration of turf was a mere half ton a month, and barley had been introduced into the loaf as a supplement to wheat. The Chamber's own level of activity was somewhat reduced in these years, and the report for 1943 noted that 'in present conditions under which legislation is applied by Orders made under the Emergency Powers Act, much of the work of the Chamber is of a temporary nature not suitable for permanent record in an Annual Report'. In January 1942 the president, Joseph Walker, interviewed various transport authorities on future prospects and suggested the building of horse-drawn wooden barges to increase the carrying capacity of the Grand Canal. After consultation with the directors of the Grand Canal Company and others, the Council decided that the government should be asked to approve and to finance the construction of such barges. In September the first pair were handed over to the Minister for Industry and Commerce who thanked the Chamber of Commerce for originating the idea. It was subsequently reported that the carrying capacity of the barges had exceeded expectations and by the end of the year eleven had been built. In April the Traffic and Transit Committee and Trade and Commerce Committee investigated the possibilities for pooling resources for retail deliveries. It was found that firms had a natural reluctance to dismiss their own employees and have their goods delivered by the employees of other firms.

However, even at this point thoughts were turning to the future, and in October 1942 the Taoiseach addressed the Chamber on post-war planning. He warned that 'state control and state intervention will tend to remain and to entrench itself in many spheres where formerly private enterprise alone held the field'. In 1943, the year in which David Coyle was president, the membership turned upwards. The question of 'post-war problems' had already been broached by the outgoing president in his address in January 1943, and in October 1943 R. J. Mortished of the International Labour Office, addressing the Chamber, warned his audience that 'when hostilities cease in Europe we shall be faced with a complex of problems that will make our war-time worries seem simple inconveniences'. In 1944 the Association of Chambers of Commerce circulated a questionnaire to endeavour to get the views of Chambers on a number of broad principles, and post-war planning was discussed again at a meeting in October 1944. War-time acceptance of legislation and of the problems of adjusting successfully to a peace-time world faced with material shortages meant that the Chamber, like businessmen generally, was prepared to take in its stride many measures which had appeared controversial less than a generation previously. One of the consequences too was that the Chamber's own view of the situation was much more sophisticated than in the past, and addresses by the president now frequently involved a close analysis of economic problems. Legislative changes involving the nationalisation of the Great Southern Railway and other major issues were taken without any traumatic reaction.

A. J. Broughton, Irish Traffic Manager, British Railways. President 1947.

Problems there were, of course. In 1947, for instance, congestion in the port of Dublin, light taxation of cooperative society profits, lightning strikes were all pressing issues of the day. But even the first of the modern bank strikes in 1950 was taken in the Chamber's stride. A relatively minor item which received a very considerable amount of attention in these years was the use and abuse of loudspeakers for advertising purposes with the Council pressing the Corporation to introduce by-laws to control their use on buildings and moving vehicles. A minor issue in 1952 harking back to the past was a vain attempt by the Chamber to prevent 'the hostelry, formerly the Bodega, from using the title "The Ouzel Galley Inn".' The early 1950s was a period when the anti-partition movement was promoted with vigour and it presented some of the rare occasions in which political issues surfaced. A resolution on the question was lost on a show of hands in May 1954. The same proposer brought the issue up again in February 1955. This time the issue was short-circuited by a proposal that the meeting proceed to the next business, which was carried on a show of hands. The vice-president, who had chaired the meeting, later explained to the press that the motion had not been rejected on its merits, but because the consideration of such a resolution was not part of the functions of a body of businessmen.

The balance of payments was the major economic preoccupation in the late 1940s. In 1954 the increase in net government borrowing was a subject of alarm, and the report for 1955 stated that 'the year to which this report refers was clearly a year of overspending'.

The increased sophistication of the Chamber's outlook and the acceptance of the State's role in economic activity were both reflected in 1951 in what became a standard feature in subsequent years: addresses to the Chamber by civil servants and heads of semi-state bodies on facets of Irish economic problems and development. In May 1951 Dr. R. C. Geary gave an address on 'Irish Statistics and some of the showings', and in October R. F. Browne, chairman of the Electricity Supply Board, addressed the meeting on 'Electricity in Industry'. In 1956 Dr. Juan Greene, chairman of the Irish Farmers' Association, was one of the speakers. These addresses and the

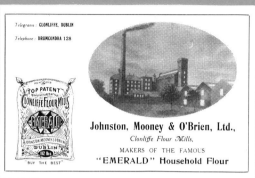

Telegrams: CLONLIFFE, DUBLIN

Telephone: DRUMCONDRA 128

TOP PATENT
CLONLIFFE FLOUR MILLS
EMERALD
JJOHNSTON MOONEY & OBRIEN
DUBLIN
112 lbs
"BUY THE BEST"

Johnston, Mooney & O'Brien, Ltd.,

Clonliffe Flour Mills,

MAKERS OF THE FAMOUS

"EMERALD" Household Flour

23

25

24

Gallaher Ltd

Cigarettes

KINGSTOWN. HARBOUR.

JACOB & C⁰ˢ
BISCUITS.

JACOB & C⁰ˢ
BISCUITS.

As a result of seventy-six years' experience of Biscuit
Manufacturing in Dublin over 200 Varieties are now
produced. They include a wide range of Assortments
of Plain and Sweet Biscuits, Afternoon Tea Specialities,
Chocolate Biscuits, Cakes and Chocolate Confectionery.

W. & R. JACOB & CO. Ltd.

BISCUIT AND CAKE MANUFACTURERS,

Established 1851.   DUBLIN.

26

Arnott & Company,

LIMITED,

WHOLESALE & RETAIL DRAPERS,

Manufacturers & Warehousemen,

—AND—

GENERAL HOUSE FURNISHERS,

DUBLIN.

N.B.—House Furnishing Guide Free on Application.

27

discussion which followed them gave both members and visitors a wide range of views in depth on Irish economic life, and also helped to create informal contact between the leading businessmen and other figures in public life.

Compared with the late 1910s and 1920s the volume of Council and Committee work was smaller but the Chamber had, after slipping in its place in the Dublin business community in the 1930s, reestablished itself as a forum for the views of the business community perhaps more effectively than ever before. The impetus to growth in membership which began in 1943 when the Chamber started to address itself to the problems both of the day and of the future maintained itself, and by 1957 the total had reached 887. It declined in the economic crisis of 1957-8 but then began a recovery which became rapid in the second half of the 1960s. No less than 300 new members were elected in 1970. The pattern of its presidency had also changed a good deal from the 1930s. Transport and shipping interests had been the most dominant, overlapping with distribution and banking. The last involvement of this group was that of David Barry in 1928 and of A. J. Broughton of the London & Midland in 1947. Industry itself, which had been poorly represented, was more significant from the time of the industrial revival in the 1930s with which the Chamber identified itself. One aspect of this was not only the emergence of some new firms from which presidents have been drawn but the re-appearance of some old ones: thus while Andrew Jameson's presidency was more a personal tribute than anything else, as he was not an active participant in the humdrum work of the Chamber, the firm of Jameson was represented again in the Presidency in 1959 with the election of Lt. Colonel J. E. Armstrong, who had the distinction of being the second member elected to honorary membership after J. C. M. Eason. Jamesons were represented again in 1974 with the election of Alec Crichton. Guinness's links with the Chamber, which had ceased to be prominent in the decades after the long presidency of the second Arthur, became closer in the post-1939 period. R. E. M. Clarke became president in 1968 and H. Hannon in 1981.

The most striking innovation in the Presidency, however, has been the growing prominence of accountancy and insurance among the professions represented, W. P. Sherriff of the Northern Assurance Company being the first to signal this new trend in 1930. Insurance was to be represented again in 1942, 1948 and 1957, Declan Lennon of Coyle, Hamilton, Hamilton and Phillips repeating the pattern in 1982. The first representative of an accountancy firm was G. Brock of Craig Gardner in 1945; he was followed in 1960 by Vincent Crowley of Kennedy, Crowley and Co., in 1976 by F. F. Carthy and in 1983 by Niall Crowley. Banking ceased in the early twentieth century to have as close an association with the Chamber as it had in the nineteenth when a pattern of interlocking directorships between the banks and the transport concerns existed. Indeed by the end of the 1910s a new strain emerged in the Chamber in a tendency to be critical of bank charges. This was to be partly smoothed over in the 1920s by the appointment of a representative of the Irish Banks' Standing Committee to a nominated post on the Council. In 1944 the appointment of David Coyle, who had been president in 1943, to a directorship in the Munster & Leinster was still something of a novelty; but the gulf has been narrowed in the last two decades by the banks frequently appointing businessmen to their boards, and the pattern is now more reminiscent of the late nineteenth-century one. Niall Crowley's presidency in 1983, that of another accountant, is the first case of a nominee of the Irish Banks' Standing Committee acceding to the presidency.

In 1957 an issue arose which was to recur frequently over the following fifteen years, and was indeed to be the main single concern of the Chamber in that period. The European Economic Community was established in 1957. Britain did not enter but put forward proposals for a European Free Trade Area, which as the Council noted were 'of serious concern to Ireland'. The creation of the European Free Trade Association gave point to this concern, but the report for 1960 at least found consolation in the fact that:

> Fears of economic isolation as a result of integrated trading between the members of the Common Market and the European Free Trade Association are somewhat allayed by the signing of an Anglo-Irish trade agreement in 1960.

The report for 1961, noting that 'the problems attendant on our entry into the Common Market and the advent of progressive free trade are without precedent in the country's economic history', welcomed the formation of the Committee on Industrial Organisation. The breakdown of Britain's negotiations for entry in 1963, the Chamber noted, did not lessen the need to continue to improve productivity, not only to expand exports but to prepare the country for the eventuality of any integrated area which might develop in the future. As the submission from the Association of Chambers of Commerce in regard to the 1962-3 budget observed: 'in the last analysis the balance of advantage will depend on the competitiveness of Irish industry; on its readiness to adopt all possible means of increasing efficiency, if necessary by concentrating on the more economic products; on its adaptability to changing patterns of trade; and on its ability to absorb any rise in costs in greater productivity'. It was to remain a theme in the 1960s which was to acquire a new significance with the reopening of negotiations in 1970. These negotiations concluded successfully with full membership on 1 January 1972. The Chamber, through the Association of Chambers of Commerce and in cooperation with the Confederation of Irish Industry and the Federated Union of Employers, opened an office in Brussels. Its report for 1971 had endorsed the outcome of the negotiations stongly:

> The Chamber of Commerce is satisfied that the Government has negotiated terms of entry to the E.E.C. which are as good as could be hoped for and better than many competent observers thought possible.

It remained sanguine about the prospects following entry:

> The full benefits of membership of the community cannot and will not be fully realised unless our own national economy is soundly based. Fundamentally it is, and there is confidence in it, as witnessed by the heavy subscriptions contributed to the Government loan in November 1972 which realised some £34 million, an unprecedented amount to be subscribed in this country to any National Loan.

Mr. P. J. Jordan was appointed as European Business Envoy and took up his position in Brussels in November 1972.

Long before Ireland was admitted to the E.E.C., industrial relations had become an increasingly insistent theme in the Chamber. Even as early as 1959 the upward movement in earnings was noted with concern: the Council observed that 'unless such an increase in wages is balanced by increased productivity, [it] must retard the efforts that are being made to reduce the country's adverse trade balance'. The address of the president at the annual general meeting in February 1962 expressed anxiety about 'this unprecedented wage drift' and especially about the fact that it was most in evidence in 'public and essential services'. In 1963 the Council was concerned about the height of the increase — 12 per cent — which had emerged in employer/trade union negotiations, and noted its preference to have 'seen increases awarded as actually warranted at the present time, and thereafter to follow the normal procedure of collective bargaining in accordance with the economic situation as it arises from time to time'. In 1964 the Council noted that the increase in productivity was well below the 12 per cent provided for in the previous year's National Agreement. It observed that some sectors in the community seemed to disregard ominously the terms of the agreement. Its concern at this stage was, however, prompted by demands for a shorter working week which were responsible for some stoppages in industry. The year 1966 seemed to provide ample justification for the fears that had been growing in the Council in the preceding years. Reporting to members on the year, it observed that:

P. J. Loughrey, President 1953.

> In May 1966 the whole commercial and industrial community was threatened with immediate closedown due to the industrial dispute in the E.S.B. At the same time no banking service was available due to the commercial banks being compelled to close as a result of strike action having been served on them by a certain section of their employees. At one time then two essential services were withdrawn from the business community.

However, all the disputes of the 1960s were entirely overshadowed in their impact by that of the maintenance men in 1969. Indeed in looking back over the decade, in the wake of this dispute, the Council even concluded that 'had the decade ended one year earlier our satisfaction in retrospect might have been, with some few exceptions, unqualified'. The maintenance strike of 1969 was characterised as 'the greatest crisis in Industrial Relations ever experienced in the history of the state', a conclusion which prefaced a long and gloomy account of industrial relations:

> It is not the function of the Chamber of Commerce to meddle in Trade Union matters or in the general field of Industrial Relations, but it would be fatuous to suggest that a Chamber of Commerce should declare itself indifferent to the overall effects of widespread industrial strife.

In its long analysis of the situation the Council observed that:

> What we saw in 1969 was a major rejection of representative authority. Members of Trade Unions refused absolutely to abide by decisions taken by their own duly appointed representatives. Employers for their part, admittedly in face of irresistible pressure, broke away from group

policy with which they had professed themselves to be in agreement. In 1970 industrial relations were even more than in 1969 the overriding preoccupation of the Chamber. Disputes in the cement industry and in the banks were the basis of concern on this occasion. The latter dispute was the main source of attention, and the Council in its report pondered on 'certain salient and sobering facts'. The first was that a country could be left without a banking system. The second was the 'enormous gap in confidence and intimacy' between the banks and the business community. The Council observed:

> Here there was frustration and annoyance, coupled with the gravest anxiety, at the complete curtain of silence and lack of communication which prevailed for the whole six month period.

Some lessons were learned by the Chamber from this dispute. When another of the interminable bank disputes blew up again in 1976 the Chamber was in a much less passive mood. When the banks closed on 25 June, the president of the Chamber, Frank Carthy, immediately called a meeting of a number of trade and professional bodies. Six meetings were held of what came to be known as the Bank Strike Committee during the duration of the dispute. Its first concern was to reduce the incidence of inconvenience to the business community. The committee's request that public servants be paid in cash was granted. It also requested that state agencies with surplus cash should pass it on to other state agencies which were short of cash to prevent it being taken out of circulation. The committee had negotiations with the Minister for Labour and with the parties to the dispute. When a solution was near the committee made it clear in correspondence to each of the associated banks that:

> The methodology adopted following the 1970 Banks Closure in calculating interest on overdrafts and terms loans was manifestly unfair in that it disregarded traditional account patterns and other relevant factors.

The much sharper and more active profile of the Chamber reflected its growing exasperation. The president chaired the meetings, and the committee's activities including deputations, no less than five press statements and a press conference were arranged through its Secretariat.

If an insistent preoccupation with industrial relations was a novelty of the Chamber's activities in the 1960s and 1970s, another was concern with the city itself and its environment. This had first emerged in the 1960s in relation to traffic congestion. No great changes in roads had taken place in central Dublin for almost a century, in fact since the 1870s and 1880s when somewhat similar problems had been to the fore. Since those years, the city had been able to cope with its problems, but they began to re-emerge in an acute form by the 1960s with the popularisation of the motor car and the sustained increase in economic activity that began at the end of the 1950s. In 1967 the Chamber sought the opinion of members on the City of Dublin Draft Development Plan, and two conferences were later held between the Traffic and Transit Committee and Corporation officials in regard to city traffic, a new Liffey bridge and approach roads to this bridge along the line of the two canals. The Council strongly supported the provision of a new river

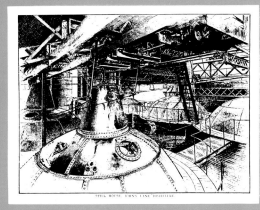

STILL HOUSE, JOHN'S LANE DISTILLERY.

31

crossing to the east of Butt Bridge, observing that:

> In the light of projections indicating that the volume of traffic on the streets of the City by 1985 will be three times greater than it is to-day, a solution to this problem can no longer be delayed.

In the following year the Council's support for what was to become the highly controversial Inner Tangent Ring Road became very evident. In 1970, despite its concern with industrial disputes which in that year's report uniquely formed the starting point of the text, the Council devoted a long section to the 'City of Dublin':

> Fifteen years ago, when few people were aware of Dublin's problems as a City, the title of a chapter such as this was likely to be a bland one such as 'The Urban Environment'. Five years later a similar chapter would have developed more bite and changed to 'Our Urban Problems'. To-day, we can give it only one title, and that with alarming immediacy, 'The Urban Crisis'. Yet each would, in reality have dealt with identical phenomena.

Traffic problems — along with improvements in public transport — have been one of the major preoccupations of the Chamber since the outset of the 1970s, and over the decade such issues took up a growing amount of the Chamber's time, as well as occupying an increasingly prominent role in its reports to the annual meetings. However in its report for 1970 the Council revealed an awareness of many other aspects of the city's problems. In 1971 the Chamber was addressed by the City Manager on 'The City of the Future'. The Council set out the traffic considerations at great length in 1972, and in at least four other years in the 1970s it was to be a major theme. However, another aspect of the city — lawlessness and vandalism — also became a major issue in the Chamber. In August 1972 a deputation was received by the Minister for Justice which included, besides members of the Chamber, representatives of the Grafton Street, Henry Street and O'Connell Street traders and four other bodies to discuss the provision of extra Guards, better equipment for them and stiffer court sentences. A long report was made to the Minister in 1975, and there were further deputations from the Chamber in 1976 and 1977. A different but not totally dissimilar preoccupation was expressed by the Chamber in 1977 and 1981; disruption of business districts by political protests.

In the course of its concern with traffic problems and lawlessness, the Council's preoccupations widened to encompass a view of the problems of the inner city. As it observed in 1974:

> It was evident to us during our conversations with those concerned with municipal planning and administration that they recognise the real danger that the city centre of Dublin will 'die' unless all those responsible for and interested in its survival generate a new pride and determination. The Chamber is a good focal point for identifying such problems and for combining the energies of the many specialised trade bodies and organisations which have the same aims.

The logical consequence of this awareness was to study the problems in a wider context. In 1978, in E. J. Kelliher's presidency, the Chamber appointed an Inner City Redevelopment Advisory Committee which in consultation with experts in social, economic and town planning drew up a report examining the problems and formulating proposals for redeveloping and revitalising the area, particularly in the fields of housing, employment, education, and youth welfare. The report was presented to both the Taoiseach and the Lord Mayor and stirred up a good deal of press interest. The Chamber had accurately anticipated one of the major concerns of recent times, as subsequent discussion and political development have shown.

In the 1970s these issues frequently took precedence over purely economic and social questions in the Chamber and they even overshadowed the issue of labour relations which had been the dominant social theme of the 1960s and of 1970 itself. Its own advisory committee on the inner city in 1978 showed a precocious awareness of issues relating to the quality of life, and indeed has been one of the factors responsible for the growing public attention to the Inner City. Yet at the same time so much of its concern had been triggered off by traffic congestion that the Chamber has seemed never to have successfully balanced its economic and social concerns. It was aware of the opposition to the Corporation's traffic plans, but in fact has never discussed the conflict inherent between some of the solutions to the traffic problems, which it has defined so accurately, and the revitalisation of the city centre. In 1980 the Council was bitterly disappointed. Not only had the Eastern By-Pass been omitted from the Development Plan, but the Inner Tangent Ring Road was retained only against considerable opposition within the City Council:

> In opposing this measure the Chamber considered that Dublin Corporation was being completely negative and indeed acting against the best interests of the City. It was recognised that this proposal was in response to the anti-road lobby which had been canvassing members of the City Council for some time on this subject.

Changes in the physical environment have always concerned the Chamber or its predecessor the Committee of Merchants, even if ironically its role has changed from one of outright opposition to change in the 1760s and 1770s to unqualified support for change in the 1970s. Dublin's physical environment is a difficult one in terms of planning. Built literally on the seashore, its port and port-related activities were and are close to the heart of the city. Hence, unlike Edinburgh and a number of other cities, it has never proved possible to segregate its historic and residential quarters from through traffic. The medieval city around Christ Church straddled the route from the later districts both of the Coombe and of Thomas Street to the port. The line of street created by the projection of Sackville Street across the new Carlisle Bridge into the two majestic streets, Westmoreland Street and D'Olier Street, one of the triumphs of Georgian planning in these islands, was subsequently commercialised at a rate which no one in the 1790s can have visualised. In other words, because of the city's physical layout, its residential districts built between the old town and the sea and straddling the newest north-south axis across the Liffey, fell prey to commerce almost as quickly as they were built. The last of Dublin's great aristocratic houses, Aldborough House, reflects the dilemma dramatically. It was built in the 1790s on the North Strand immediately beyond the recently created Gardiner Street which swept from Mountjoy Square, newest of the city's squares, to the custom house, the most

T. F. Laurie, President 1954.

magnificent of its public buildings. Within a few years its immediate environment began to deteriorate. The problem of reconciling the flow of traffic with the preservation of the character and amenity of the city is not easy. Central Dublin in recent centuries has never had a stable character: as new districts have been spawned, within existing districts a three-fold sequence of residential use, commercialisation and decay repeated itself. The conflict has been reflected in the Chamber as it addressed itself to different issues. In 1976 in connection with the draft development plan it favoured relaxation of the planning laws:

> On the matter of conservation the use of powers extended to the planning authority to restore, preserve and protect buildings should only be used after full and possibly public examination of the economic consequences to both occupier and the Community. Also that should the Community decide to preserve property and thereby restrain normal development it should be expected to pay for it.

Two years previously in its report for 1974 the Council took a much broader view:

> Dublin is a beautifully situated city with magnificent architecture. The enhancing of natural and inherited advantages is important from every point of view, including the furtherance of business. In this area there is virtually unlimited scope for improvement. The Chamber is one place in which all Dublin citizens concerned with any aspect of commerce can come together and play their part in helping to make Dublin a better place in which to live and work.

And indeed, in noting that the city had 'many natural and acquired scenic and architectural advantages', the Council observed that 'many of these advantages are being lost through lack of planning, by vandalism, traffic congestion, etc.; all of which results from underrating our inheritance and from comparative disinterest in the future'.

An issue which came up in 1981 was the re-organisation of local government. The Council's forthright views in the 1920s had been responsible for the reform of the Corporation and it also supported strongly the revision of the city boundaries in the 1930s. On this occasion, when its views were sought in 1981 along with those of other bodies by the Minister for the Environment, they were no less forthright:

> In summary it appears to the Chamber of Commerce that a completely new structure of local administration is required in the metropolitan area. Existing boundaries, whether urban or county, should be disregarded. The only means by which an objective review and objective recommendation can be achieved is through a tribunal similar to that which was led by the late George Gavan Duffy in the 1930s. The Chamber of Commerce recommends that such a body be set up and required to report within a specified period. It is necessary that the new bodies when created be capable of surviving as long a period of reluctance by Parliament to make decisions in politically difficult areas.

On the macro-economic front, the balance of payments had been the recurrent worry of the Chamber in the 1950s. In the 1961 report however the Council was able to observe that 'over the past five years a considerable increase in the output of exportable goods has taken place. During that time our balance of payments position has been only slightly in deficit, and indeed on one occasion in surplus'. In the 1960s concern shifted to rising prices associated with wage claims. The 1963 report noted that the turnover tax in increasing retail prices had triggered off wage demands. By the early 1970s the concern with inflation was a marked one. It is striking, however, that the Council failed to appreciate the full implications of the rise in energy prices: it entailed a real transfer of resources on a permanent basis from the oil consumers to the oil producers, a fact which reduced the resources available for allocation to other uses, however desirable. Hence the implications were that all future planning and expectations should be scaled down by the proportion of this transfer. In failing to draw this conclusion the Chamber of course was making the same mistake as the Government and public opinion at large, both of whom failed to advert to the consequences for future policy. This was very evident again in 1978 when the government drew up its green paper on 'Full Employment' on the basis of very optimistic assumptions, and the Chamber's observations conveyed to the Minister for Economic Planning seemed too sanguine, welcoming the Paper as confirmation of 'the confidence with which the Government undertook its task of revitalisation of the national effort.' The Chamber however did not fail to make the point that borrowings for the purpose of financing current expenditure should be reduced. But uncharacteristically, the Council in its budget submission in November 1978 with the forthcoming budget in mind, relaxed its objection to the high level of borrowing. It noted that if the government reduced borrowing from 13.5 per cent of Gross National Product to 10.5 per cent:

> This reduction would be a blow to confidence for investment. This Association submits that whilst unnecessary increase in borrowing ought to be avoided by the Government, restraint in incomes should be the main weapon used by the Government to avoid heavy tax increases. This would give the economy a much needed opportunity to expand and permit of borrowing reduction in future years.

The Chamber's business has become much more complex since 1945. In the past, while the presidency was a busy office, it was possible for a president to describe it, as did J. J. Halpin in 1932 as 'a liberal education'. But increasingly in the post-1945 world the Chamber's concerns have become technical rather than broadly economic or political. The Council foresaw this in its report for 1945:

> Members should continue their endeavours to secure additional members so that the influence of the Chamber on the numerous problems arising in post-war conditions may be further strengthened. The Chamber's activities have widened considerably in recent years and will grow in importance to every businessman by reason of the increasing complexity of trade and legislation affecting trade.

This was confirmed by the experience of subsequent years, and the range and sophistication of the Chamber's interests widened markedly. The

complexity became much greater in the 1960s and 1970s, especially as PAYE, turnover tax and finally, on entry to the EEC, Value Added Tax, were introduced. At the same time legislation on income and company tax became increasingly complex. In sharp contrast to the pre-1939 years, these issues now took up much of the Chamber's time. A deputation to the Minister with a submission ahead of the budget had become commonplace, and there was frequently a follow-up submission on the detail of the Finance Bill. All this meant a large amount of detailed study and argument. In its 1978 report the Council put on record its appreciation of the professional assistance which it received free of charge from Stokes, Kennedy Crowley & Co. and Craig Gardner & Co., advice which was crucial to the Taxation Committee and to the Trade & Commerce Committee in the preparation of their submissions. The Chamber was now involved in helping its members in a large number of ways in dealing with these problems. For instance, in connection with the introduction of Value Added Tax, the Chamber organised an afternoon

The newly restored and redecorated council chamber at 7, Clare Street.

121

seminar for its members for the purpose of discussing with the Revenue Commissioners the practicalities of operating the tax. The meeting was attended by 350 members and was addressed by the Chairman of the Revenue Commissioners and by the Principal Inspector in the V.A.T. office of the Commissioners, The Chamber's journal frequently carried articles on matters of technical or practical value to its readers.

The Chamber has changed dramatically over time. As an organisation it addresses itself to a wider range of problems, often on a continuing basis. Moreover, its role has become much more clear-cut, that of dealing with problems common to all business, leaving it to separate interests to pursue more sectional issues. Its function in this regard has been repeatedly emphasised by its officers and has come to be recognised within the business community. Its role as a general voice for the business community, avoiding issues which could divide businessmen themselves, was not always evident in the past. In fact, in its early decades, direct rivalries between businessmen influenced its development: while religious and political considerations separated the Pims and their supporters from the Guinness group in the Chamber, there were also business rivalries which can be dimly perceived and which sharpened this conflict. In the 1810s for instance, when Guinness ran foul of some of Dublin opinion, some agitation was mounted to encourage people to switch to Pim's ale. Throughout the nineteenth century the port and its administration remained the main continuing interest of the Chamber: this did not always serve as a unifying bond, and there was frequently a conflict of interest between shipowner members and trading members, especially on the controversial question of how port revenue should be raised. These divisions militated against the Chamber's success. Its membership moved uncertainly over time: stasis and fall in the middle decades of the nineteenth century very pointedly reflecting its lack of hold on the loyalties of businessmen. On the other hand, when there was a greater sense of common purpose, its membership could rise, as in the third quarter of the century when the Chamber escaped from its narrow domination by Arthur Guinness, or again in the decade before the first world war when a more cohesive attitude among businessmen began to develop. In the 1920s, too, faced with the problems of adaptation to the novel conditions of the Free State, membership rose, just as in the 1930s complacency led to a sizeable decline both in numbers and vigour.

Two specific features have helped the modern Chamber to develop a sustained appeal. First, as life has become more complex, the range of issues before it has increased. Businessmen thus find themselves with more in common, whereas when the issues were few, either their interest was sustained only in periods of great enthusiasm or anxiety, or the dominant issues could divide as well as bring them together. Secondly, the membership of the Chamber has changed. Superficially it is little larger than at its peak at the end of a sustained expansion in the third quarter of the nineteenth century; but much of the membership at that time consisted of private individuals or professional men, in some cases concerned with the business interests of the city only in a general way. Few of the members of the modern Chamber come from this category; they are mostly active businessmen often expressly representing the interests or areas covered by

BRINDLEYS LIMITED
LETTERPRESS & LITHOGRAPHIC
PRINTERS.

GOODBODY'S

38

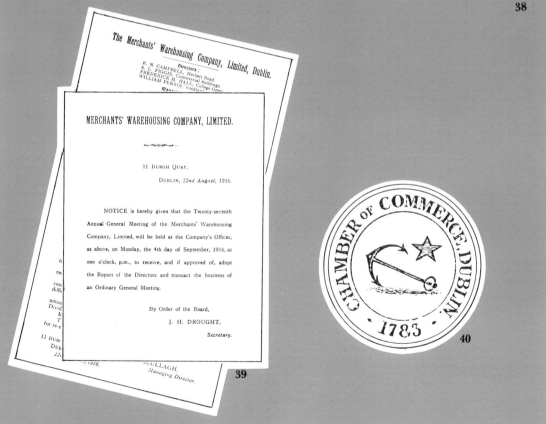

The Merchants' Warehousing Company, Limited, Dublin.

Directors :
R. N. CAMPBELL, Herbert Road.
A. L. FIGGIS, Commercial Buildings.
FREDERICK H. HALL, College Green.
WILLIAM PERRIN, Rockland Grove.
Man...

MERCHANTS' WAREHOUSING COMPANY, LIMITED.

11 BURGH QUAY,

DUBLIN, 22nd August, 1916.

NOTICE is hereby given that the Twenty-seventh
Annual General Meeting of the Merchants' Warehousing
Company, Limited, will be held at the Company's Offices,
as above, on Monday, the 4th day of September, 1916, at
one o'clock, p.m., to receive, and if approved of, adopt
the Report of the Directors and transact the business of
an Ordinary General Meeting.

By Order of the Board,

J. H. DROUGHT,

Secretary.

39

CHAMBER of COMMERCE. DUBLIN.
· 1783 ·

40

their company or firm. An associated change has been that officers, especially in recent decades, have been active businessmen, usually at the peak of their business careers. In the nineteenth and early twentieth centuries some of the Chamber's influential figures came from outside the main stream of business, or were elderly or retired businessmen. This is a pattern vestiges of which can be traced as late as the 1930s, and it is a factor which helped to account for the intermittent quality of the Chamber's drive. Indeed, its modern presidents have each had his own style, and interesting differences in emphasis can be detected from one presidency to another amid the general momentum of the Chamber's ongoing concerns.

A major internal change occurred in 1964, breaking a thread of continuity going back to 1805. The lease on the premises in Commercial Buildings running out and it not being possible to renew it, the present premises in Clare Street were acquired. The Chamber's membership grew over the 1970s from 1010 in 1971 to 1300 at the end of the decade, exceeding its nineteenth century peak, and virtually double the membership over the greater part of its history. Over the two centuries of its existence the Chamber has had ups and downs, including its collapse in two periods, after 1793 and again for several years before 1820. The success of its role from the early 1900s onwards has been unprecedented in its history. It has steered clear of the controversies which sometimes weakened it in the past, and it has established itself firmly not only as a voice of businessmen in issues of general concern but also as a vehicle of close contact between the business world and the State. This has imparted some degree of routine to its work in comparison to the fitful pattern of growth and decline in the past. Less of the work is done in Council and more in Committee than in the 1920s or preceding periods. It has acquired, however, a weight in the consideration of economic matters which would be the envy of the handful of determined men who in 1783 and again in 1820 sought to gain for businessmen some voice in affairs that affected them.

Presidents

1783-1788	TRAVERS HARTLEY
†1805	JOSEPH WILSON
†1805	ALDERMAN NATHANIEL HONE
†1805	JOHN DUNCAN
†1806	WILLIAM HONE
†1806	RANDAL MACDONNELL
†1806	BARTHOLOMEW MAZIERE
†1807	GEORGE CARLETON
1820-1822	JOSHUA PIM
1823-1826	LELAND CROSTHWAIT
‡1827-1856	ARTHUR GUINNESS
1857-1870	THOMAS CROSTHWAIT
1871-1881	WILLIAM DIGGES LA TOUCHE
1882-1884	JOHN BAGOT
1885-1887	SIR RICHARD MARTIN BART.
1888-1890	JOHN LLOYD BLOOD
1891-1893	MICHAEL MURPHY
1894-1896	JOHN R. WIGHAM
1897-1899	SIR JOHN E. BARRY
1900-1902	SIR J. MALCOLM INGLIS
1903-1904	SIR JAMES MURPHY BART.
1905-1906	MARCUS GOODBODY
1907-1908	LAURENCE MALONE
1909-1911	JOHN MOONEY
1912-1913	WILLIAM M. MURPHY
*1914	RICHARD K. GAMBLE
1915	PATRICK LEONARD
1916	RICHARD W. BOOTH
1917	MATTHEW J. MINCH
1918	EDWARD H. ANDREWS
1919	WILLIAM WALLACE
1920	JOHN GOOD
1921	RIGHT HON. ANDREW JAMESON
1922	WILLIAM HEWAT
1923	JAMES SHANKS
1924	W. LOMBARD MURPHY
1925	WILLIAM CROWE
1926	GEORGE N. JACOB
1927	J. C. M. EASON
1928	DAVID BARRY
1929	SENATOR SIR WALTER NUGENT BART.
1930	W. P. SHERRIFF
1931	JAMES J. HALPIN
1932	D. J. COGAN
1933	H. M. DOCKRELL
1934	EDGAR ANDERSON
1935	ALDERMAN J. HUBBARD CLARK
1936	JOHN O'NEILL
1937	FRANK A. LOWE
1938	THOMAS F. LAURIE
1939	W. WOODS HILL
1940	A. A. BRUNKER
1941	JOSEPH WALKER
1942	J. HAROLD AYLWARD
1943	DAVID COYLE
1944	ALD. ERNEST E. BENSON
1945	G. BROCK
1946	JOHN HAWKINS
1947	A. J. BROUGHTON
1948	S. V. KIRKPATRICK
1949	GEORGE WATSON
1950	SENATOR F. M. SUMMERFIELD
1951	M. P. ROWAN
1952	G. H. C. CRAMPTON
1953	PATRICK J. LOUGHREY
1954	THOMAS F. LAURIE
1955	STEPHEN MACKENZIE
1956	ALEX O'D. SHIEL

†*The constitution did not provide for presidents in these years, only for 'chairmen' elected for shorter periods.*

‡*No president was elected for 1856, a vice president Thomas Crosthwait acting as the Chamber's head until the annual general meeting of 1857.*

**The Articles of Association were revised this year and, in accordance with the new provisions, Presidents are not eligible for re-election to that office until a period of a year from retirement has elapsed.*

1957 J. W. GALLAGHER	1971 JAMES A. WALMSLEY
1958 J. HAROLD DOUGLAS	1972 M. W. O'REILLY
1959 LT. COL. J. E. ARMSTRONG	1973 JAMES GALLAGHER
1960 VINCENT CROWLEY	1974 A. C. CRICHTON
1961 JOHN O'BRIEN	1975 H. J. BAMBRICK
1962 PHILIP R. WALKER	1976 F. F. CARTHY
1963 THOMAS C. LENEHAN	1977 ALD. P. F. BELTON
1964 THOMAS F. LAURIE	1978 E. J. KELLIHER
1965 E. C. G. MULHERN	1979 J. A. LENEHAN
1966 J. R. DICK	1980 H. C. TIERNEY
1967 JAMES BOYLAN	1981 H. HANNON
1968 R. E. M. CLARKE	1982 D. L. LENNON
1969 GERALD L. M. WHEELER	1983 NIALL CROWLEY
1970 EDWARD W. BECK	

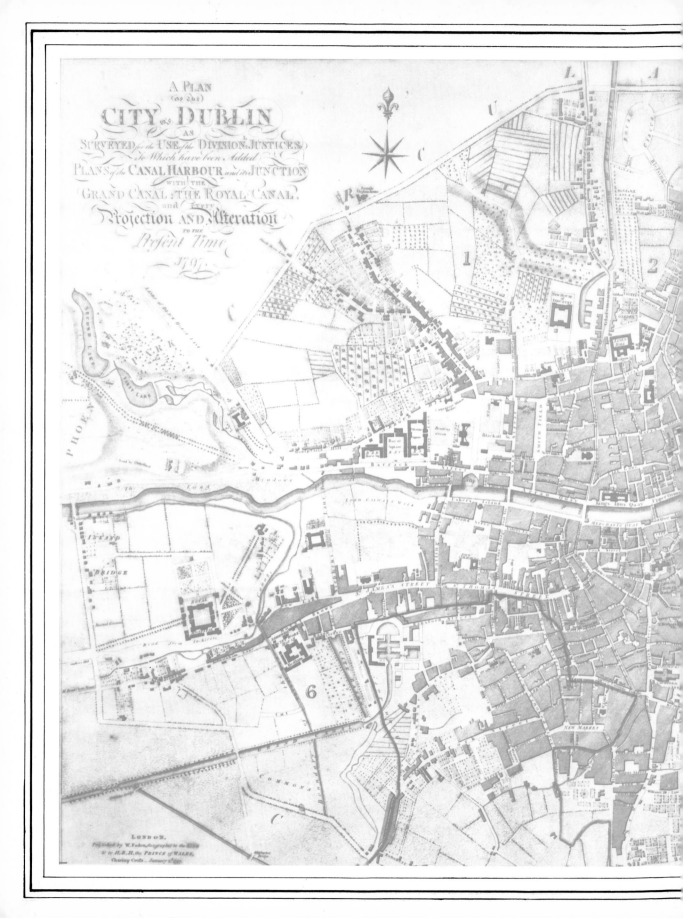